THE HUNCHBACK

James Sheridan Knowles

The Hunchback

James Sheridan Knowles

© 1st World Library – Literary Society, 2004
PO Box 2211
Fairfield, IA 52556
www.1stworldlibrary.org
First Edition

LCCN: 2004091225

Softcover ISBN: 1-59540-663-8
eBook ISBN: 1-59540-763-4

Purchase *"The Hunchback"*
as a traditional bound book at:
www.1stWorldLibrary.org/purchase.asp?ISBN=1-59540-663-8

1st World Library Literary Society is a nonprofit organization dedicated to promoting literacy by:

- Creating a free internet library accessible from any computer worldwide.
- Hosting writing competitions and offering book publishing scholarships.

Readers interested in supporting literacy through sponsorship, donations or membership please contact:
literacy@1stworldlibrary.org
Check us out at: www.1stworldlibrary.org

The Hunchback
*contributed by the Mahaney Family
in support of
1st World Library Literary Society*

INTRODUCTION

James Sheridan Knowles was born at Cork in 1784, and died at Torquay in December, 1862, at the age of 78. His father was a teacher of elocution, who compiled a dictionary, and who was related to the Sheridans. He moved to London when his son was eight years old, and there became acquainted with William Hazlitt and Charles Lamb. The son, after his school education, obtained a commission in the army, but gave up everything for the stage, and made his first appearance at the Crow Street Theatre, in Dublin. He did not become a great actor, and when he took to writing plays he did not prove himself a great poet, but his skill in contriving situations through which a good actor can make his powers tell upon the public, won the heart of the great actor of his day, and as Macready's own poet he rose to fame.

Before Macready had discovered him, Sheridan Knowles lived partly by teaching elocution at Belfast and Glasgow, partly by practice of elocution as an actor. In 1815 he produced at the Belfast Theatre his first play, Caius Gracchus. His next play, Virginius was produced at Glasgow with great success. Macready, who had, at the age of seventeen, begun his career as an actor at his father's theatre in Birmingham, had, on Monday, October 5th, 1819, at the age of twenty-six, taken the Londoners by storm in the character of Richard III Covent Garden reopened its closed treasury. It was promptly followed by a success in Coriolanus, and Macready's place was made. He was at once offered fifty pounds a night for appearing on one evening a week at Brighton. It was just after that turn in Macready's fortunes that a friend at Glasgow recommended to him the part of Virginius in Sheridan Knowles's play lately produced there. He agreed unwillingly to look at it, and says that in April, 1820, the parcel containing the MS. came as he was going out. He hesitated, then sat down to read it that he might get a wearisome job over. As he read, he says, "The freshness and simplicity of the dialogue fixed my attention; I read on and on, and was soon absorbed in the interest of the story and the passion of its scenes, till at its close I found myself in such a state of excitement that for a time I was undecided what step to take. Impulse was in the ascendant, and snatching up my pen I hurriedly wrote, as my agitated feelings prompted, a letter to the author, to me then a perfect stranger." Bryan Procter (Barry Cornwall) read the play next day with Macready, and confirmed him in his admiration of it.

Macready at once got it accepted at the theatre, where nothing was spent on scenery, but there was a good cast, and the enthusiasm of Macready as stage manager for the occasion half affronted some of his seniors. On the 17th of May, 1820, about a month after it came into Macready's hands, Virginius was produced at Covent Garden, where, says the actor in his "Reminiscences," "the curtain fell amidst the most deafening applause of a highly-excited auditory." Sheridan Knowles's fame, therefore, was made, like that of his friend Macready, and the friendship between author and actor continued. Sheridan Knowles had a kindly simplicity of character, and the two qualities for which an actor most prizes a dramatist, skill in providing opportunities for acting that will tell, and readiness to make any changes that the actor asks for. The postscript to his first letter to Macready was, "Make any alterations you like in any part of the play, and I shall be obliged to you." When he brought to the great actor his play of William Tell - Caius Gracchus had been produced in November, 1823 - there were passages of writing in it that stopped the course of action, and, says Macready, "Knowles had less of the tenacity of authorship than most writers," so that there was no difficulty about alterations, Macready having in a very high degree the tenacity of actorship. And so, in 1825, Tell became another of Macready's best successes.

Sheridan Knowles continued to write for the stage until 1845, when he was drawn wholly from the theatre by a religious enthusiasm that caused him, in 1851, to essay the breaking of a lance with Cardinal Wiseman on the subject of Transubstantiation. Sir Robert Peel gave ease to his latter days by a pension of 200 pounds a year from the Civil List, which he had honourably earned by a career as dramatist, in which he sought to appeal only to the higher sense of literature, and to draw enjoyment from the purest source. Of his plays time two comedies {1} here given are all that have kept their place upon the stage. As one of the most earnest dramatic writers of the present century he is entitled to a little corner in our memory. Worse work of the past has lasted longer than the plays of Sheridan Knowles are likely to last through the future.

H. M.

THE HUNCHBACK.

DRAMATIS PERSONAE.
(AS ORIGINALLY PERFORMED AT COVENT GARDEN IN 1832.)

Julia	Miss F. KEMBLE.
Helen	Miss TAYLOR.
Master Walter	Mr. J. S. KNOWLES.
Sir Thomas Clifford	Mr. C. KEMBLE.
Lord Tinsel	Mr. WRENCH.
Master Wilford	Mr. J. MASON.
Modus	Mr. ABBOTT.
Master Heartwell	Mr. EVANS.
Gaylove	Mr. HENRY.
Fathom	Mr. MEADOWS.
Thomas	Mr. BARNES.
Stephen	Mr. PAYNE.
Williams	Mr. IRWIN.
Simpson	Mr. BRADY.
Waiter	Mr. HEATH.
Holdwell	Mr. BENDER.
Servants	{ Mr. J. COOPER.
	{ Mr. LOLLETT.

ACT I.

SCENE I. - A Tavern.

On one side SIR THOMAS CLIFFORD, at a table, with wine before him; on the other, MASTER WILFORD, GAYLOVE, HOLDWELL, and SIMPSON, likewise taking wine.

Wilf. Your wine, sirs! your wine! You do not justice to mine host of the Three Tuns, nor credit to yourselves; I swear the beverage is good! It is as palatable poison as you will purchase within a mile round Ludgate! Drink, gentlemen; make free. You know I am a man of expectations; and hold my money as light as the purse in which I carry it.

Gay. We drink, Master Wilford. Not a man of us has been chased as yet.

Wilf. But you fill not fairly, sirs! Look at my measure! Wherefore a large glass, if not for a large draught? Fill, I pray you, else let us drink out of thimbles! This will never do for the friends of the nearest of kin to the wealthiest peer in Britain.

Gay. We give you joy, Master Wilford, of the prospect of advancement which has so unexpectedly opened to you.

Wilf. Unexpectedly indeed! But yesterday arrived the news that the Earl's only son and heir had died; and today has the Earl himself been seized with a mortal illness. His dissolution is looked for hourly; and I, his cousin in only the third degree, known to him but to be unnoticed by him - a decayed gentleman's son - glad of the title and revenues of a scrivener's clerk - am the undoubted successor to his estates and coronet.

Gay. Have you been sent for?

Wilf. No; but I have certified to his agent, Master Walter, the Hunchback, my existence, and peculiar propinquity; and momentarily expect him here.

Gay. Lives there anyone that may dispute your claim - I mean vexatiously?

Wilf. Not a man, Master Gaylove. I am the sole remaining branch of the family tree.

Gay. Doubtless you look for much happiness from this change of fortune?

Wilf. A world! Three things have I an especial passion for. The finest hound, the finest horse, and the finest wife in the kingdom, Master Gaylove!

Gay. The finest wife?

Wilf. Yes, sir; I marry. Once the earldom comes into my line, I shall take measures to perpetuate its remaining there. I marry, sir! I do not say that I shall love. My heart has changed mistresses too often to settle down in one servitude now, sir. But fill, I pray you, friends. This, if I mistake not, is the day whence I shall date my new fortunes; and, for that reason, hither have I invited you, that, having been so long my boon companions, you shall be the first to congratulate me.

[Enter Waiter]

Waiter. You are wanted, Master Wilford.

Wilf. By whom?

Waiter. One Master Walter.

Wilf. His lordship's agent! News, sirs! Show him in!

[Waiter goes out]

My heart's a prophet, sirs - The Earl is dead.

[Enter MASTER WALTER]

Well, Master Walter. How accost you me?

Wal. As your impatience shows me you would have me. My Lord, the Earl of Rochdale!

Gay. Give you joy!

Hold. All happiness, my lord!

Simp. Long life and health unto your lordship!

Gay. Come! We'll drink to his lordship's health! 'Tis two o'clock, We'll e'en carouse till midnight! Health, my lord!

Hold. My lord, much joy to you!

Simp. All good to your lordship!

Wal. Give something to the dead!

Gay. Give what?

Wal. Respect! He has made the living! First to him that's gone, Say "Peace!" - and then with decency to revels!

Gay. What means the knave by revels?

Wal. Knave?

Gay. Ay, knave!

Wal. Go to! Thou'rt flushed with wine!

Gay. Thou sayest false! Though didst thou need a proof thou speakest true, I'd give thee one. Thou seest but one lord here, And I see two!

Wal. Reflect'st thou on my shape? Thou art a villain!

Gay. [Starting up.] Ha!

Wal. A coward, too! Draw!

[Drawing his sword.]

Gay. Only mark him! how he struts about! How laughs his straight sword at his noble back.

Wal. Does it? It cuffs thee for a liar then!

[Strikes GAYLOVE with his sword.]

Gay. A blow!

Wal. Another, lest you doubt the first!

Gay. His blood on his own head! I'm for you, sir!

[Draws.]

Clif. Hold, sir! This quarrel's mine!

[Coming forward and drawing.]

Wal. No man shall fight for me, sir!

Clif. By your leave, Your patience, pray! My lord, for so I learn Behoves me to accost you - for your own sake Draw off your friend!

Wal. Not till we have a bout, sir!

Clif. My lord, your happy fortune ill you greet! Ill greet it those who love you - greeting thus The herald of it!

Wal. Sir, what's that to you? Let go my sleeve!

Clif. My lord, if blood be shed On the fair dawn of your prosperity, Look not to see the brightness of its day. 'Twill be o'ercast throughout!

Gay. My lord, I'm struck!

Clif. You gave the first blow, and the hardest one! Look, sir; if swords you needs must measure, I'm Your mate, not he!

Wal. I'm mate for any man!

Clif. Draw off your friend, my lord, for your own sake!

Wilf. Come, Gaylove! let's have another room.

Gay. With all my heart, since 'tis your lordship's will.

Wilf. That's right! Put up! Come, friends!

[WILFORD and Friends go out.]

Wal. I'll follow him! Why do you hold me? 'Tis not courteous of you! Think'st thou I fear them? Fear! I rate them but As dust! dross! offals! Let me at them! - Nay, Call you this kind? then kindness know I not; Nor do I thank you for't! Let go, I say!

Clif. Nay, Master Walter, they're not worth your wrath.

Wal. How know you me for Master Walter? By My hunchback, eh! - my stilts of legs and arms, The fashion more of ape's than man's? Aha! So you have heard them, too - their savage gibes As I pass on, - "There goes my lord!" aha! God made me, sir, as well as them and you. 'Sdeath! I demand of you, unhand me, sir!

Clif. There, sir, you're free to follow them! Go forth, And I'll go too: so on your wilfulness Shall fall whate'er of evil may ensue. Is't fit you waste your choler on a burr? The nothings of the town; whose sport it is To break their villain jests on worthy men, The graver still the fitter! Fie for shame! Regard what such would say? So would not I, No more than heed a cur.

Wal. You're right, sir; right, For twenty crowns! So there's my rapier up! You've done me a good turn against my will; Which, like a wayward child, whose pet is off, That made him restive under wholesome check, I now right humbly own, and thank you for.

Clif. No thanks, good Master Walter, owe you me! I'm glad to know you, sir.

Wal. I pray you, now, How did you learn my name? Guessed I not right? Was't not my comely hunch that taught it you?

Clif. I own it.

Wal. Right, I know it; you tell truth. I like you for't.

Clif. But when I heard it said That Master Walter was a worthy man, Whose word would pass on 'change soon as his bond; A liberal man - for schemes of public good That sets down tens, where others units write; A charitable man - the good he does, That's told of, not the half; I never more Could see the hunch on Master Walter's back!

Wal. You would not flatter a poor citizen?

Clif. Indeed, I flatter not!

Wal. I like your face - A frank and honest one! Your frame's well knit, Proportioned, shaped!

Clif. Good sir!

Wal. Your name is Clifford - Sir Thomas Clifford. Humph! You're not the heir Direct to the fair baronetcy? He That was, was drowned abroad. Am I not right? Your cousin, was't not? - so succeeded you To rank and wealth, your birth ne'er promised you.

Clif. I see you know my history.

Wal. I do. You're lucky who conjoin the benefits Of penury and abundance; for I know Your father was a man of slender means. You do not blush, I see. That's right! Why should you? What merit to be dropped on fortune's hill? The honour is to mount it. You'd have done it; For you were trained to knowledge, industry, Frugality, and honesty, - the sinews That surest help the climber to the top, And keep him there. I have a clerk, Sir Thomas, Once served your father; there's the riddle for you. Humph! I may thank you for my life to-day.

Clif. I pray you say not so.

Wal. But I will say so! Because I think so, know so, feel so, sir! Your fortune, I have heard, I think, is ample! And doubtless you live up to't?

Clif. 'Twas my rule, And is so still, to keep my outlay, sir, A span within my means.

Wal. A prudent rule! The turf is a seductive pastime!

Clif. Yes.

Wal. You keep a racing stud? You bet?

Clif. No, neither. 'Twas still my father's precept -

"Better owe A yard of land to labour, than to chance Be debtor for a rood!"

Wal. 'Twas a wise precept. You've a fair house - you'll get a mistress for it?

Clif. In time!

Wal. In time! 'Tis time thy choice were made. Is't not so yet? Or is thy lady love The newest still thou seest?

Clif. Nay, not so. I'd marry, Master Walter, but old use - For since the age of thirteen I have lived In the world - has made me jealous of the thing That flattered me with hope of profit. Bargains Another would snap up, might be for me: Till I had turned and turned them! Speculations, That promised, twenty, thirty, forty, fifty, Ay, cent-per-cent. returns, I would not launch in, When others were afloat, and out at sea; Whereby I made small gains, but missed great losses. As ever, then, I looked before I leaped, So do I now.

Wal. Thou'rt all the better for it! Let's see! Hand free - heart whole - well-favoured - so! Rich, titled! Let that pass! - kind, valiant, prudent - Sir Thomas, I can help thee to a wife, Hast thou the luck to win her!

Clif. Master Walter! You jest!

Wal. I do not jest. I like you! mark - I like you, and I like not everyone! I say a wife, sir, can I help you to, The pearly texture of whose dainty skin Alone were worth thy baronetcy! Form And feature has she, wherein move and glow The charms, that in the marble, cold and still, Culled by the sculptor's jealous skill and joined there, Inspire us! Sir, a maid, before whose feet, A duke - a duke might lay his coronet, To lift her to his state, and partner her! A fresh heart too! - a young fresh heart, sir; one That Cupid has not toyed with, and a warm one - Fresh, young, and warm! mark that! a mind to boot; Wit, sir; sense, taste; - a garden strictly tended - Where nought but what is costly flourishes! A consort for a king, sir! Thou shalt see her!

Clif. I thank you, Master Walter! As you speak, Methinks I see me at the altar-foot! Her hand fast locked in mine! - the ring put on! My wedding-bell rings merry in my ear; And round me throng glad tongues that give me joy To be the bridegroom of so fair a bride!

Wal. What! sparks so thick? We'll have a blaze anon!

Servant. [Entering.] The chariot's at the door.

Wal. It waits in time! Sir Thomas, it shall bear thee to the bower Where dwells this fair - for she's no city belle, But e'en a sylvan goddess!

Clif. Have with you!

Wal. You'll bless the day you served the Hunchback, sir!

[They go out.]

SCENE II. - A Garden before a Country House.

[Enter JULIA and HELEN.]

Helen. I like not, Julia, this your country life. I'm weary on't!

Julia. Indeed? So am not I! I know no other; would no other know!

Helen. You would no other know! Would you not know Another relative? - another friend - Another house - another anything, Because the ones you have already please you? That's poor content! Would you not be more rich, More wise, more fair? The song that last you learned You fancy well; and therefore shall you learn No other song? Your virginal, 'tis true, Hath a sweet tone; but does it follow thence, You shall not have another virginal? You may, love, and a sweeter one; and so A sweeter life may find than this you lead!

Julia. I seek it not. Helen, I'm constancy!

Helen. So is a cat, a dog, a silly hen, An owl, a bat, - where they are wont to lodge That still sojourn, nor care to shift their quarters. Thou'rt constancy? I am glad I know thy name! The spider comes of the same family, That in his meshy fortress spends his life, Unless you pull it down and scare him from it. And so thou'rt constancy? Ar't proud of that? I'll warrant thee I'll match thee with a snail From year to year that never leaves his house! Such constancy forsooth! - a constant grub That houses ever in the self-same nut Where he was born, till hunger drives him out, Or plunder breaketh through his castle wall! And so, in very deed, thou'rt constancy!

Julia. Helen, you know the adage of the tree; - I've ta'en the bend. This rural life of mine, Enjoined me by an unknown father's will, I've led from infancy. Debarred from hope Of change, I ne'er have sighed for change. The town To me was like the moon, for any thought I e'er should visit it - nor was I schooled To think it half so fair!

Helen. Not half so fair! The town's the sun, and thou hast dwelt in night E'er since thy birth, not to have seen the town! Their women there are queens, and kings their men; Their houses palaces!

Julia. And what of that? Have your town-palaces a hall like this? Couches so fragrant? walls so high-adorned? Casements with such festoons, such prospects, Helen, As these fair vistas have? Your kings and queens! See me a May-day queen, and talk of them!

Helen. Extremes are ever neighbours. 'Tis a step From one to the other! Were thy constancy A reasonable thing - a little less Of constancy - a woman's constancy - I should not wonder wert thou ten years hence The maid I know thee now; but, as it is, The odds are ten to one, that this day year Will see our May-day queen a city one!

Julia. Never! I'm wedded to a country life: O, did you hear what Master Walter says! Nine times in ten the town's a hollow thing, Where what things are is nought to what they show; Where merit's name laughs merit's self to scorn! Where friendship and esteem that ought to be The tenants of men's hearts, lodge in their looks And tongues alone. Where little virtue, with A costly keeper, passes for a heap; A heap for none that has a homely one! Where fashion makes the law - your umpire which You bow to, whether it has brains or not! Where Folly taketh off his cap and bells, To clap on Wisdom, which must bear the jest! Where to pass current you must seem the thing, The passive thing, that others think; and not Your simple, honest, independent self!

Helen. Ay: so says Master Walter. See I not What can you find in Master Walter, Julia, To be so fond of him!

Julia. He's fond of me! I've known him since I was a child. E'en then, The week I thought a weary, heavy one, That brought not Master Walter. I had those About me then that made a fool of me, As children oft are fooled; but more I loved Good Master Walter's lesson than the play With which they'd surfeit me. As I grew up, More frequent Master Walter came, and more I loved to see him! I had tutors then, Men of great skill and learning - but not one That taught like Master Walter. What they'd show me, And I, dull as I was, but doubtful saw, - A word from Master Walter made as clear As daylight! When my schooling days were o'er -That's now good three years past - three years - I vow I'm twenty, Helen! - well, as I was saying, When I had done with school, and all were gone, Still Master Walter came! and still he comes,

Summer or winter - frost or rain! I've seen The snow upon a level with the hedge, Yet there was Master Walter!

Helen. Who comes here? A carriage, and a gay one - who alights? Pshaw! Only Master Walter! What see you, Which thus repairs the arch of the fair brow, A frown was like to spoil? - A gentleman! One of our town kings! Mark! - How say you now? Wouldst be a town queen, Julia? Which of us, I wonder, comes he for?

Julia. For neither of us; He's Master Walter's clerk, most like.

Helen. Most like! Mark him as he comes up the avenue; So looks a clerk! A clerk has such a gait! So does a clerk dress, Julia! - mind his hose - They're very like a clerk's! a diamond loop And button, note you, for his clerkship's hat, - O, certainly a clerk! A velvet cloak, Jerkin of silk, and doublet of the same, - For all the world a clerk! See, Julia, see, How Master Walter bows, and yields him place, That he may first go in - a very clerk! I'll learn of thee, love, when I'd know a clerk!

Julia. I wonder who he is!

Helen. Wouldst like to know? Wouldst for a fancy ride to town with him? I prophesy he comes to take thee thither!

Julia. He ne'er takes me to town! No, Helen, no! To town who will, a country life for me!

Helen. We'll see!

[Enter FATHOM.]

Fath. You're wanted, madam.

Julia. [Embarrassed.] Which of us?

Fath. You, madam.

Helen. Julia! what's the matter? Nay, Mount not the rose so soon! He must not see it A month hence. 'Tis loves flower, which once she wears, The maid is all his own.

Julia. Go to!

Helen. Be sure He comes to woo thee! He will bear thee hence; He'll make thee change the country for the town.

Julia. I'm constancy. Name he the town to me, I'll tell what I think on't!

Helen. Then you guess He comes a wooing?

Julia. I guess nought.

Helen. You do! At your grave words, your lips, more honest, smile, And show them to be traitors. Hie to him.

Julia. Hie thee to soberness.

[Goes out.]

Helen. Ay, will I, when, Thy bridemaid, I shall hie to church with thee. Well, Fathom, who is come?

Fath. I know not.

Helen. What! Didst thou not hear his name?

Fath. I did.

Helen. What is't?

Fath. I noted not.

Helen. What hast thou ears for, then?

Fath. What good were it for me to mind his name? I do but what I must do. To do that Is labour quite enough!

Wal. [Without.] What, Fathom!

Fath. Here.

Wal. [Entering.] Here, sirrah! Wherefore didst not come to me?

Fath. You did not bid me come.

Wal. I called thee.

Fath. Yes. And I said "Here;" and waited then to know Your worship's will with me.

Wal. We go to town. Thy mistress, thou, and all the house.

Fath. Well, sir?

Wal. Mak'st thou not ready then to go to town?

Hence, knave, despatch!

[FATHOM goes out.]

Helen. Go we to town?

Wal. We do; 'Tis now her father's will she sees the town.

Helen. I'm glad on't. Goes she to her father?

Wal. No: At the desire of thine she for a term shares roof with thee.

Helen. I'm very glad on't.

Wal. What! You like her, then? I thought you would. 'Tis time She sees the town.

Helen. It has been time for that These six years.

Wal. By thy wisdom's count. No doubt You've told her what a precious place it is.

Helen. I have.

Wal. I even guessed as much. For that I told thee of her; brought thee here to see her; And prayed thee to sojourn a space with her; That its fair space, from thy too fair report, Might strike a novice less - so less deceive her. I did not put thee under check.

Helen. 'Twas right, - Else had I broken loose, and run the wilder! So knows she not her father yet: that's strange. I prithee how does mine?

Wal. Well - very well. News for thee.

Helen. What?

Wal. Thy cousin is in town.

Helen. My cousin Modus?

Wal. Much do I suspect That cousin's nearer to thy heart than blood.

Helen. Pshaw! Wed me to a musty library! Love him who nothing loves but Greek and Latin! But, Master Walter, you forget the main Surpassing point of all! Who's come with you?

Wal. Ay, that's the question!

Helen. Is he soldier or Civilian? lord or gentleman? He's rich, If that's his chariot! Where is his estate? What brings it in? Six thousand pounds a year? Twelve thousand, may be! Is he bachelor, Or husband? Bachelor I'm sure he is Comes he not hither wooing, Master Walter? Nay, prithee, answer me!

Wal. Who says thy sex Are curious? That they're patient, I'll be sworn; And reasonable - very reasonable - To look for twenty answers in a breath! Come, thou shalt be enlightened - but propound Thy questions one by one! Thou'rt far too apt A scholar! My ability to teach Will ne'er keep pace, I fear, with thine to learn.

[They go out.]

SCENE III. - An Apartment in the House.

[Enter JULIA, followed by CLIFFORD.]

Julia. No more! I pray you, sir, no more!

Clif. I love you!

Julia. You mock me, sir!

Clif. Then is there no such thing On earth as reverence; honour filial, the fear Of kings, the awe of supreme heaven itself, Are only shows and sounds that stand for nothing. I love you!

Julia. You have known me scarce a minute!

Clif. Say but a moment, still I say I love you! Love's not a flower that grows on the dull earth; Springs by the calendar; must wait for the sun - For rain; - matures by parts; - must take its time To stem, to leaf, to bud, to blow. It owns A richer soil, and boasts a quicker seed! You look for it, and see it not; and lo! E'en while you look, the peerless flower is up. Consummate in the birth!

Julia. Is't fear I feel? Why else should beat my heart? It can't be fear! Something I needs must say. You're from the town; How comes it, sir, you seek a country wife? Methinks 'twill tax his wit to answer that.

Clif. In joining contrasts lieth love's delight. Complexion, stature, nature, mateth it, Not with their kinds, but with their opposites. Hence hands of snow in palms of russet lie; The form of Hercules affects the sylph's; And breasts, that case the lion's fear-proof heart, Find their meet lodge in arms where tremors dwell! Haply for this, on Afric's swarthy neck, Hath Europe's priceless pearl been seen to hang, That makes the orient poor! So with degrees, Rank passes by the circlet-graced brow, Upon the forehead, bare, of notelessness To print the nuptial kiss. As with degrees So is't with habits; therefore I, indeed A gallant of the town, the town forsake, To win a country wife.

Julia. His prompt reply My backward challenge shames! Must I give o'er? I'll try his wit again. Who marries me Must lead a country life.

Clif. The life I'd lead! But fools would fly from it; for O! 'tis sweet! It finds the heart out, be there one to find; And corners in't where store of pleasures lodge, We never dreamed were there! It is to dwell 'Mid smiles that are not neighbours to deceit; Music, whose melody is of the heart; And gifts, that are not made for interest, - Abundantly bestowed by Nature's cheek, And voice, and hand! It is to live on life, And husband it! It is to constant scan The handiwork of Heaven. It is to con Its mercy, bounty, wisdom, power! It is To nearer see our God!

Julia. How like he talks To Master Walter! Shall I give it o'er? Not yet. Thou wouldst not live one half a year! A quarter mightst thou for the novelty Of fields and trees; but then it needs must be In summer time, when they go dressed.

Clif. Not it! In any time - say winter! Fields and trees Have charms for me in very winter time.

Julia. But snow may clothe them then.

Clif. I like them full As well in snow!

Julia. You do?

Clif. I do.

Julia. But night Will hide both snow and them, and that sets in Ere afternoon is out. A heavy thing, A country fireside in a winter's night, To one bred in the town, - where winter's said, For sun of gaiety and sportiveness, To beggar shining summer.

Clif. I should like A country winter's night especially!

Julia. You'd sleep by the fire.

Clif. Not I; I'd talk to thee.

Julia. You'd tire of that!

Clif. I'd read to thee.

Julia. And that!

Clif. I'd talk to thee again.

Julia. And sooner tire Than first you did, and fall asleep at last. You'd never do to lead a country life.

Clif. You deal too harshly with me! Matchless maid, As loved instructor brightens dullest wit, Fear not to undertake the charge of me! A willing pupil kneels to thee, and lays His title and his fortune at your feet.

Julia. His title and his fortune!

[Enter MASTER WALTER and HELEN. - JULIA, disconcerted, retires with the latter. - CLIFFORD rises.]

Wal. So, Sir Thomas! Aha! you husband time! Well, was I right? Is't not the jewel that I told you 'twas? Wouldst thou not give thine eyes to wear it? Eh? It has an owner, though, - nay, start not, - one That may be bought to part with't, and with whom I'll stand thy friend - I will - I say, I will! A strange man, sir, and unaccountable: But I can humour him - will humour him For thy sake, good Sir Thomas; for I like thee. Well, is't a bargain? Come, thy hand upon it. A word or two with thee.

[They retire. JULIA and HELEN come forward.]

Julia. Go up to town!

Helen. Have I not said it ten times o'er to thee? But if thou likest it not, protest against it.

Julia. Not if 'tis Master Walter's will.

Helen. What then? Thou wouldst not break thy heart for Master Walter?

Julia. That follows not!

Helen. What follows not?

Julia. That I Should break my heart, because we go to town.

Helen. Indeed? - Oh, that's another matter. Well, I'd e'en advise thee then to do his will; And, ever after, when I prophesy, Believe me, Julia!

[They retire. MASTER WALTER comes forward.]

[Enter FATHOM.]

Fath. So please you, sir, a letter, - a post-haste letter! The bearer on horseback, the horse in a foam - smoking like a boiler at the heat - be sure a posthaste letter!

Wal. Look to the horse and rider.

[Opens the letter and reads.]

What's this? A testament addressed to me, Found in his lordship's escritoire, and thence Directed to be taken by no hand But mine. My presence instantly required.

[SIR THOMAS, JULIA, and HELEN come forward.]

Come, my mistresses, You dine in town to-day. Your father's will, It is, my Julia, that you see the world; And thou shalt see it in its best attire. Its gayest looks - its richest finery It shall put on for thee, that thou may'st judge Betwixt it, and this rural life you've lived. Business of moment I'm but thus advised of, Touching the will of my late noble master, The Earl of Rochdale, recently deceased, Commands me for a time to leave thee there. Sir Thomas, hand her to the chariot. Nay, I tell thee true. We go indeed to town!

[They go out.]

ACT II.

SCENE I. - An Apartment in Master Heartwell's House.

[Enter FATHOM and THOMAS.]

Thos. Well, Fathom, is thy mistress up?

Fath. She is, Master Thomas, and breakfasted.

Thos. She stands it well! 'Twas five, you say, when she came home; and wants it now three-quarters of an hour of ten? Wait till her stock of country health is out.

Fath. 'Twill come to that, Master Thomas, before she lives another month in town! three, four, five six o'clock are now the hours she keeps. 'Twas otherwise with her in the country. There, my mistress used to rise what time she now lies down.

Thos. Why, yes; she's changed since she came hither.

Fath. Changed, do you say, Master Thomas? Changed, forsooth! I know not the thing in which she is not changed, saving that she is still a woman. I tell thee there is no keeping pace with her moods. In the country she had none of them. When I brought what she asked for, it was "Thank you, Fathom," and no more to do; but now, nothing contents her. Hark ye! were you a gentleman, Master Thomas, - for then you know you would be a different kind of man, - how many times would you have your coat altered?

Thos. Why, Master Fathom, as many times as it would take to make it fit me.

Fath. Good! But, supposing it fitted thee at the first?

Thos. Then would I have it altered not at all.

Fath. Good! Thou wouldst be a reasonable gentleman. Thou wouldst have a conscience. Now hark to a tale about my lady's last gown. How many times, think you, took I it back to the sempstress?

Thos. Thrice, may be.

Fath. Thrice, may be! Twenty times, may be; and not a turn too many, for the truth on't. Twenty times, on the oath of the sempstress. Now mark me - can you count?

Thos. After a fashion.

Fath. You have much to be thankful for, Master Thomas. You London serving-men have a world of things, which we in the country never dream of. Now mark:- Four times took I it back for the flounce; twice for the sleeves; three for the tucker - How many times in all is that?

Thos. Eight times to a fraction, Master Fathom.

Fath. What a master of figures you are! Eight times - now recollect that! And then found she fault with the trimmings. Now tell me, how many times took I back the gown for the trimmings?

Thos. Eight times more, perhaps!

Fath. Ten times to a certainty. How many times makes that?

Thos. Eighteen, Master Fathom, by the rule of addition.

Fath. And how many times more will make twenty?

Thee. Twice, by the same rule.

Fath. Thou hast worked with thy pencil and slate, Master Thomas! Well, ten times, as I said, took I back the gown for the trimmings; and was she content after all? I warrant you no, or my ears did not pay for it. She wished, she said, that the slattern sempstress had not touched the gown, for nought had she done but botched it. Now what think you had the sempstress done to the gown?

Thos. To surmise that, I must be learned in the sempstress's art.

Fath. The sempstress's art! Thou hast hit it! Oh, the sweet sempstress! the excellent sempstress! Mistress of her scissors and needles, which are pointless and edgeless to her art! The sempstress had done nothing to the gown; yet raves and storms my mistress at her for having botched it in the making and mending; and orders her straight to make another one, which home the sempstress brings on Tuesday last.

Thos. And found thy fair mistress as many faults with that?

Fath. Not one! She finds it a very pattern of a gown! A well-sitting flounce! The sleeves a fit - the tucker a fit - the trimmings her fancy to a T - ha! ha! ha! and she praised the sempstress - ha! ha! ha! and she smiles at me, and I smile - ha! ha! ha! and the sempstress smiles - ha! ha! ha! Now, why did the sempstress smile?

Thos. That she had succeeded so well in her art.

Fath. Thou hast hit it again! The jade must have been born a sempstress! If ever I marry, she shall work for my wife. The gown was the same gown, and there was my mistress's twentieth mood!

Thos. What think you will Master Walter say when he comes back? I fear he'll hardly know his country maid again. Has she yet fixed her wedding-day?

Fath. She has, Master Thomas. I coaxed it from her maid. She marries, Monday week.

Thos. Comes not Master Walter back to-day?

Fath. Your master expects him. [A ringing.] Perhaps that's he. I prithee go and open the door; do, Master Thomas, do; for proves it my master, he'll surely question me.

Thos. And what should I do?

Fath. Answer him, Master Thomas, and make him none the wiser. He'll go mad, when he learns how my lady flaunts it! Go! open the door, I prithee. Fifty things, Master Thomas, know you, for one thing that I know! You can turn and twist a matter into any other kind of matter; and then twist and turn it back again, if needs be; so much you servants of the town beat us of the country, Master Thomas. Open the door, now; do, Master Thomas, do!

[They go out.]

SCENE II. - A Garden with two Arbours.

[Enter MASTER HEARTWELL and MASTER WALTER meeting.]

Heart. Good Master Walter, welcome back again!

Wal. I'm glad to see you, Master Heartwell!

Heart. How, I pray you, sped the mighty business which So sudden called you hence?

Wal. Weighty, indeed! What thou wouldst ne'er expect - wilt scarce believe! Long-hidden wrong, wondrously come to light, And great right done! But more of this anon. Now of my ward discourse! Likes she the town? How does she? Is she well? Canst match me her Among your city maids?

Heart. Nor court ones neither! She far outstrips them all!

Wal. I knew she would. What else could follow in a maid so bred? A pure mind, Master Heartwell! - not a taint From intercourse with the distempered town; With which all contact was walled out, until, Matured in soundness, I could trust her to it, And sleep amidst infection!

Heart. Master Walter!

Wal. Well?

Heart. Tell me, prithee, which is likelier To plough a sea in safety? - he that's wont To sail in it, - or he that by the chart Is master of its soundings, bearings, - knows Is headlands, havens, currents - where 'tis bold, And where behoves to keep a good look-out. The one will swim, where sinks the other one?

Wal. The drift of this?

Heart. Do you not guess it?

Wal. Humph!

Heart. If you would train a maid to live in town, Breed her not in the country!

Wal. Say you so? And stands she not the test?

Heart. As snow stands fire! Your country maid has melted all away, And plays the city lady to the height; Her mornings gives to mercers, milliners, Shoemakers, jewellers, and haberdashers; Her noons, to calls; her afternoons, to dressing; Evenings, to plays and drums; and nights, to routs, Balls, masquerades! Sleep only ends the riot, Which waking still begins!

Wal. I'm all amaze! How bears Sir Thomas this?

Heart. Why, patiently; Though one can see with pain.

Wal. She loves him? Ha! That shrug is doubt! She'd ne'er consent to wed him Unless she loved him! -

never! Her young fancy The pleasures of the town - new things - have caught, Anon their hold will slacken; she'll become Her former self again; to its old train Of sober feelings will her heart return; And then she'll give it wholly to the man Her virgin wishes chose!

Heart. Here comes Sir Thomas; And with him Master Modus.

Wal. Let them pass: I would not see him till I speak with her.

[They retire into one of the Arbours.]

[Enter CLIFFORD and MODUS.]

Clif. A dreadful question is it, when we love, To ask if love's returned! I did believe Fair Julia's heart was mine - I doubt it now! But once last night she danced with me, her hand, To this gallant and that engaged, as soon As asked for? Maid that loved would scarce do this? Nor visit we together as we used, When first she came to town. She loves me less Than once she did - or loves me not at all.

Mod. I'm little skilled, Sir Thomas, in the world: What mean you now to do?

Clif. Remonstrate with her; Come to an understanding, and, at once, If she repents her promise to be mine, Absolve her from it - and say farewell to her.

Mod. Lo, then, your opportunity - she comes - My cousin also: - her will I engage, Whilst you converse together.

Clif. Nay, not yet! My heart turns coward at the sight of her. Stay till it finds new courage! Let them pass.

[CLIFFORD and MODUS retire into the other Arbour.]

[Enter JULIA and HELEN.]

Helen. So, Monday week will say good morn to thee A maid, and bid good night a sober wife!

Julia. That Monday week, I trust, will never come, That brags to make a sober wife of me!

Helen. How changed you are, my Julia!

Julia. Change makes change.

Helen. Why wedd'st thou, then?

Julia. Because I promised him!

Helen. Thou lovest him?

Julia. Do I?

Helen. He's a man to love! A right well-favoured man!

Julia. Your point's well favoured. Where did you purchase it? In Gracechurch Street?

Helen. Pshaw! never mind my point, but talk of him.

Julia. I'd rather talk with thee about the lace. Where bought you it? In Gracechurch Street, Cheapside, Whitechapel, Little Britain? Can't you say Where 'twas you bought the lace?

Helen. In Cheapside, then. And now, then, to Sir Thomas! He is just The height I like a man.

Julia. Thy feather's just The height I like a feather! Mine's too short! What shall I give thee in exchange for it?

Helen. What shall I give thee for a minute's talk About Sir Thomas?

Julia. Why, thy feather.

Helen. Take it!

Clif. [Aside to Modus.] What, likes she not to speak of me?

Helen. And now Let's talk about Sir Thomas - much I'm sure He loves you.

Julia. Much I'm sure, he has a right! Those know I who would give their eyes to be Sir Thomas, for my sake!

Helen. Such too, know I. But 'mong them none that can compare with him, Not one so graceful.

Julia. What a graceful set Your feather has!

Helen. Nay, give it back to me, Unless you pay me for't.

Julia. What was't to get?

Helen. A minute's talk with thee about Sir Thomas.

Julia. Talk of his title, and his fortune then.

Clif. [Aside.] Indeed! I would not listen, yet I must!

Julia. An ample fortune, Helen - I shall be A happy wife! What routs, what balls, what masques, What gala-days!

Clif. [Aside.] For these she marries me! She'll talk of these!

Julia. Think not, when I am wed, I'll keep the house as owlet does her tower, Alone, - when every other bird's on wing. I'll use my palfrey, Helen; and my coach; My barge, too, for excursion on the Thames: What drives to Barnet, Hackney, Islington! What rides to Epping, Hounslow, and Blackheath! What sails to Greenwich, Woolwich, Fulham, Kew! I'll set a pattern to your lady wives!

Clif. [Aside.] Ay, lady? Trust me, not at my expense.

Julia. And what a wardrobe! I'll have change of suits For every day in the year! and sets for days! My morning dress, my noon dress, dinner dress, And evening dress! Then will I show you lace A foot deep, can I purchase; if not, I'll specially bespeak it. Diamonds too! Not buckles, rings, and earrings only - but Whole necklaces and stomachers of gems! I'll shine! be sure I will.

Clif. [Aside.] Then shine away; Who covets thee may wear thee; - I'm not he!

Julia. And then my title! Soon as I put on The ring, I'm Lady Clifford. So I take Precedence of plain mistress, were she e'en The richest heiress in the land! At town Or country ball, you'll see me take the lead, While wives that carry on their backs the wealth To dower a princess, shall give place to me; - Will I not profit, think you, by my right? Be sure I will! marriage shall prove to me A never-ending pageant. Every day Shall show how I am spoused! I will be known For Lady Clifford all the city through, And fifty miles the country round about. Wife of Sir Thomas Clifford, baronet - Not perishable knight - who, when he makes A lady of me, doubtless must expect To see me play the part of one.

Clif. [Coming forward.] Most true; But not the part which you design to play.

Julia. A listener, sir!

Clif. By chance, and not intent, Your speech was forced upon mine ear, that ne'er More thankless duty to my heart discharged! Would for that heart it ne'er had known the sense Which tells it 'tis a bankrupt, there, where most It coveted to be rich, and thought it was so! O Julia, is it you? Could I have set A coronet upon that stately brow, Where partial nature hath already bound A brighter circlet - radiant beauty's own - I had been proud to see thee proud of it, So for the donor thou hadst ta'en the gift, Not for the gift ta'en him. Could I have poured The wealth of richest Croesus in thy lap, I had been blest to see thee scatter it, So I was still thy riches paramount!

Julia. Know you me, sir!

Clif. I do. On Monday week We were to wed - and are - so you're content; The day that weds, wives you to be widowed. Take The privilege of my wife; be Lady Clifford! Outshine the title in the wearing on't! My coffers, lands, all are at thy command; Wear all! but, for myself, she wears not me, Although the coveted of every eye, Who would not wear me for myself alone.

Julia. And do you carry it so proudly, sir?

Clif. Proudly, but still more sorrowfully, lady! I'll lead thee to the church on Monday week. Till then, farewell and then, farewell for ever! O Julia, I have ventured for thy love, As the bold merchant, who, for only hope Of some rich gain, all former gains will risk. Before I asked a portion of thy heart, I perilled all my own; and now, all's lost!

[CLIFFORD and MODUS go out.]

Julia. Helen!

Helen. What ails you, sweet?

Julia. I cannot breathe - quick, loose my girdle, oh!

[Faints.]

[MASTER WALTER and MASTER HEARTWELL come forward.]

Wal. Good Master Heartwell, help to take her in, Whilst I make after him! and look to her! Unlucky chance that took me out of town!
[They go out severally.]

SCENE III. - The Street.

[Enter CLIFFORD and STEPHEN, meeting.]

Ste. Letters, Sir Thomas.

Clif. Take them home again, I shall not read them now.

Ste. Your pardon, sir, But here is one directed strangely.

Clif. How?

Ste. "To Master Clifford, gentleman, now styled Sir Thomas Clifford, baronet."

Clif. Indeed! Whence comes that letter?

Ste. From abroad.

Clif. Which is it?

Ste. So please you, this, Sir Thomas.

Clif. Give it me.

Ste. That letter brings not news to wish him joy upon. If he was disturbed before, which I guessed by his looks he was, he is not more at ease now. His hand to his head! A most unwelcome letter! If it brings him news of disaster, fortune does not give him his deserts; for never waited servant upon a kinder master.

Clif. Stephen!

Ste. Sir Thomas!

Clif. From my door remove The plate that bears my name.

Ste. The plate, Sir Thomas!

Clif. The plate - collect my servants and instruct them To make out each their claims, unto the end Of their respective terms, and give them in To my steward. Him and them apprise, good fellow, That I keep house no more. As you go home, Call at my coachmaker's and bid him stop The carriage I bespoke. The one I have Send with my horses to the mart whereat Such things are sold by auction. They're for sale; Pack up my wardrobe, have my trunks conveyed To the inn in the next street; and when that's done, Go round my tradesmen and collect their bills, And bring them to me at the inn.

Ste. The inn!

Clif. Yes; I go home no more. Why, what's the matter? What has fallen out to make your eyes fill up? You'll get another place. I'll certify You're honest and industrious, and all That a servant ought to be.

Ste. I see, Sir Thomas, Some great misfortune has befallen you?

Clif. No! I have health; I have strength; my reason, Stephen, and A heart that's clear in truth, with trust in God. No great disaster can befall the man Who's still possessed of these! Good fellow, leave me. What you would learn, and have a right to know, I would not tell you now. Good Stephen, hence! Mischance has fallen on me - but what of that? Mischance has fallen on many a better man. I prithee leave me. I grow sadder while I see the eye with which you view my grief. 'Sdeath, they will out! I would have been a man, Had you been less a kind and gentle one. Now, as you love me, leave me.

Ste. Never master So well deserved the love of him that served him.

[STEPHEN goes out.]

Clif. Misfortune liketh company; it seldom Visits its friends alone. Ha! Master Walter, And ruffled too. I'm in no mood for him.

[Enter MASTER WALTER.]

Wal. So, Sir - Sir Thomas Clifford! what with speed And choler - I do gasp for want of breath.

Clif. Well, Master Walter?

Wal. You're a rash young man, sir; Strong-headed and wrong-headed, and I fear, sir, Not over delicate in that fine sense Which men of honour pride themselves upon!

Clif. Well, Master Walter?

Wal. A young woman's heart, sir, Is not a stone to carve a posy on! Which knows not what is writ on't; which you may buy, Exchange, or sell, sir, keep or give away, sir: It is a richer - yet a poorer thing; Priceless to him that owns and prizes it; Worthless, when owned, not prized; which makes the man That covets it, obtains it, and discards it - A fool, if not a villain, sir.

Clif. Well, sir?

Wal. You never loved my ward, sir!

Clif. The bright Heavens Bear witness that I did!

Wal. The bright Heavens, sir, Bear not false witness. That you loved her not Is clear - for had you loved her, you'd have plucked Your heart from out your breast, ere cast her from your heart! Old as I am, I know what passion is. It is the summer's heat, sir, which in vain We look for frost in. Ice, like you, sir, knows But little of such heat! We are wronged, sir, wronged! You wear a sword, and so do I.

Clif. Well, sir!

Wal. You know the use, sir, of a sword?

Clif. I do. To whip a knave, sir, or an honest man! A wise man or a fool - atone for wrong, Or double the amount on't! Master Walter, Touching your ward, if wrong is done, I think On my side lies the grievance. I would not say so Did I not think so. As for love - look, sir, That hand's a widower's, to its first mate sworn To clasp no second one. As for amends, sir, You're free to get them from a man in whom You've been forestalled by fortune, for the spite Which she has vented on him, if you still Esteem him worth your anger. Please you read That letter. Now, sir, judge if life is dear To one so much a loser.

Wal. What, all gone! Thy cousin living they reported dead!

Clif. Title and land, sir, unto which add love! All gone, save life and honour, which, ere I'll lose, I'll let the other go.

Wal. We're public here, And may be interrupted. Let us seek Some spot of privacy. Your letter, sir.

[Gives it back.]

Though fortune slights you, I'll not slight you; not Your title or the lack of it I heed. Whether upon the score of love or hate, With you and you alone I settle, sir. We've gone too far. 'Twere folly now to part Without a reckoning.

Clif. Just as you please.

Wal. You've done A noble lady wrong.

Clif. That lady, sir, Has done me wrong.

Wal. Go to, thou art a boy Fit to be trusted with a plaything, not A woman's heart. Thou knowest not what it is! And that I'll prove to thee, soon as we find Convenient place. Come on, sir! you shall get A lesson that shall serve you for the rest Of your life. I'll make you own her, sir, a piece Of Nature's handiwork, as costly, free From bias, flaw, and fair, as ever yet Her cunning hand turned out. Come on, sir! come!

[They go out.]

ACT III.

SCENE I. - A Drawing-room.

[ENTER LORD TINSEL and the EARL OF ROCHDALE.]

Tin. Refuse a lord! A saucy lady this. I scarce can credit it.

Roch. She'll change her mind. My agent, Master Walter, is her guardian.

Tin. How can you keep that Hunchback in his office? He mocks you.

Roch. He is useful. Never heed him. My offer now do I present through him. He has the title-deeds of my estates, She'll listen to their wooing. I must have her. Not that I love her, but that all allow She's fairest of the fair.

Tin. Distinguished well! 'Twere most unseemly for a lord to love! - Leave that to commoners! 'Tis vulgar - she's Betrothed, you tell me, to Sir Thomas Clifford?

Roch. Yes.

Tin. That a commoner should thwart a lord! Yet not a

commoner. A baronet Is fish and flesh. Nine parts plebeian, and Patrician in the tenth. Sir Thomas Clifford! A man, they say, of brains! I abhor brains As I do tools: they're things mechanical. So far are we above our forefathers They to their brains did owe their titles, as Do lawyers, doctors. We to nothing owe them, Which makes us far the nobler.

Roch. Is it so?

Tin. Believe me. You shall profit by my training; You grow a lord apace. I saw you meet A bevy of your former friends, who fain Had shaken hands with you. You gave them fingers! You're now another man. Your house is changed - Your table changed - your retinue - your horse - Where once you rode a hack, you now back blood; - Befits it, then, you also change your friends!

[Enter WILLIAMS.]

Will. A gentleman would see your lordship.

Tin. Sir! What's that?

Will. A gentleman would see his lordship.

Tin. How know you, sir, his lordship is at home? Is he at home because he goes not out? He's not at home, though there you see him, sir; Unless he certify that he's at home! Bring up the name of the gentleman, and then Your lord will know if he's at home or not.

[WILLIAMS goes out.]

Your man was porter to some merchant's door, Who

never taught him better breeding Than to speak the vulgar truth! Well, sir?

[WILLIAMS having re-entered.]

Will. His name, So please your lordship, Markham.

Tin. Do you know The thing?

Roch. Right well! I'faith a hearty fellow, Son to a worthy tradesman, who would do Great things with little means; so entered him In the Temple. A good fellow, on my life. Nought smacking of his stock!

Tin. You've said enough! His lordship's not at home.

[WILLIAMS goes out.]

We do not go By hearts, but orders! Had he family - Blood - though it only were a drop - his heart Would pass for something; lacking such desert, Were it ten times the heart it is, 'tis nought!

[Enter WILLIAMS.]

Will. One Master Jones hath asked to see you lordship.

Tin. And what was your reply to Master Jones?

Will. I knew not if his lordship was at home.

Tin. You'll do. Who's Master Jones?

Roch. A curate's son.

Tin. A curate's! Better be a yeoman's son! Was it the rector's son, he might be known, Because the rector is a rising man, And may become a bishop. He goes light, The curate ever hath a loaded back! He may be called the yeoman of the church, That sweating does his work, and drudges on, While lives the hopeful rector at his ease. How made you his acquaintance, pray?

Roch. We read Latin and Greek together.

Tin. Dropping them - As, now that you're a lord, of course you've done - Drop him - You'll say his lordship's not at home.

Will. So please your lordship, I forgot to say, One Richard Cricket likewise is below.

Tin. Who? - Richard Cricket! You must see him, Rochdale! A noble little fellow! A great man, sir! Not knowing whom, you would be nobody! I won five thousand pounds by him!

Roch. Who is he? I never heard of him.

Tin. What! never heard Of Richard Cricket! - never heard of him! Why, he's the jockey of Newmarket; you May win a cup by him, or else a sweepstakes. I bade him call upon you. You must see him. His lordship is at home to Richard Cricket.

Roch. Bid him wait in the ante-room.

[WILLIAMS goes out.]

Tin. The ante-room! The best room in your house!

You do not know The use of Richard Cricket! Show him, sir, Into the drawing-room. Your lordship needs Must keep a racing stud, and you'll do well To make a friend of Richard Cricket. Well, sir: What's that?

[Enter WILLIAMS.]

Will. So please your lordship, a petition.

Tin. Hadst not a service 'mongst the Hottentots Ere thou camest hither, friend? Present thy lord With a petition! At mechanics' doors, At tradesmen's, shopkeepers', and merchants' only, Have such things leave to knock! Make thy lord's gate A wicket to a workhouse! Let us see it - Subscriptions to a book of poetry! Cornelius Tense, M.A. Which means he construes Greek and Latin, works Problems in mathematics, can chop logic, And is a conjurer in philosophy, Both natural and moral. - Pshaw! a man Whom nobody, that is anybody, knows! Who, think you, follows him? Why, an M.D., An F.R.S., an F.AS., and then A D.D., Doctor of Divinity, Ushering in an LL.D., which means Doctor of Laws - their harmony, no doubt, The difference of their trades! There's nothing here But languages, and sciences, and arts. Not an iota of nobility! We cannot give our names. Take back the paper, And tell the bearer there's no answer for him:- That is the lordly way of saying "No." But, talking of subscriptions, here is one To which your lordship may affix your name.

Roch. Pray, who's the object?

Tin. A most worthy man! A man of singular deserts; a man In serving whom your lordship will serve me, - Signor Cantata.

Roch. He's a friend of yours?

Tin. Oh, no, I know him not! I've not that pleasure. But Lady Dangle knows him; she's his friend, He will oblige us with a set of concerts, Six concerts to the set. - The set, three guineas. Your lordship will subscribe?

Roch. Oh, by all means.

Tin. How many sets of tickets? Two at least. You'll like to take a friend? I'll set you down Six guineas to Signor Cantata's concerts, And now, my Lord, we'll to him; then we'll walk.

Roch. Nay, I would wait the lady's answer.

Tin. Wait! take an excursion to the country; let Her answer wait for you!

Roch. Indeed!

Tin. Indeed! Befits a lord nought like indifference. Say an estate should fall to you, you'd take it As it concerned more a stander by Than you. As you're a lord, be sure you ever Of that make little other men make much of; Nor do the thing they do, but the right contrary. Where the distinction else 'twixt them and you?

[They go out.]

SCENE II. - An Apartment in Master Heartwell's House.

[MASTER WALTER discovered looking through title-deeds and papers.]

Wal. So falls out everything, as I would have it, Exact in place and time. This lord's advances Receives she, - as, I augur, in the spleen Of wounded pride she will, - my course is clear. She comes - all's well - the tempest rages still.

[JULIA enters, and paces the room in a state of high excitement.]

Julia. What have my eyes to do with water? Fire Becomes them better!

Wal. True!

Julia. Yet, must I weep To be so monitored, and by a man! A man that was my slave! whom I have seen Kneel at my feet from morn till noon, content With leave to only gaze upon my face, And tell me what he read there, - till the page I knew by heart, I 'gan to doubt I knew, Emblazoned by the comment of his tongue! And he to lesson me! Let him come here On Monday week! He ne'er leads me to church! I would not profit by his rank, or wealth, Though kings might call him cousin, for their sake! I'll show him I have pride!

Wal. You're very right!

Julia. He would have had to-day our wedding-day! I fixed a month from this. He prayed and prayed; I dropped a week. He prayed and prayed the more! I dropped a second one. Still more he prayed! And I took off another week, - and now I have his leave to wed, or not to wed! He'll see that I have pride!

Wal. And so he ought.

Julia. O! for some way to bring him to my foot! But he should lie there! Why, 'twill go abroad That he has cast me off. That there should live The man could say so! Or that I should live To be the leavings of a man!

Wal. Thy case I own a hard one!

Julia. Hard? 'Twill drive me mad! His wealth and title! I refused a lord - I did! - that privily implored my hand, And never cared to tell him on't! So much I hate him now, that lord should not in vain Implore my hand again!

Wal. You'd give it him?

Julia. I would.

Wal. You'd wed that lord?

Julia. That lord I'd wed; - Or any other lord, - only to show him That I could wed above him!

Wal. Give me your hand And word to that.

Julia. There! Take my hand and word!

Wal. That lord hath offered you his hand again.

Julia. He has?

Wal. Your father knows it: he approves of him. There are the title-deeds of the estates, Sent for my jealous scrutiny. All sound, - No flaw, or speck, that e'en the lynx-eyed law Itself could find. A lord of many lands! In Berkshire half a county; and the same In Wiltshire, and in Lancashire! Across The Irish Sea a principality! And not a rood with bond or lien on it! Wilt give that lord a wife? Wilt make thyself A countess? Here's the proffer of his hand. Write thou content, and wear a coronet!

Julia. [Eagerly.] Give me the paper.

Wal. There! Here's pen and ink. Sit down. Why do you pause? A flourish of The pen, and you're a countess.

Julia. My poor brain Whirls round and round! I would not wed him now, Were he more lowly at my feet to sue Than e'er he did!

Wal. Wed whom?

Julia. Sir Thomas Clifford.

Wal. You're right.

Julia. His rank and wealth are roots to doubt; And

while they lasted, still the weed would grow, Howe'er you plucked it. No! That's o'er - that's done. Was never lady wronged so foul as I! [Weeps.]

Wal. Thou'rt to be pitied.

Julia. [Aroused.] Pitied! Not so bad As that.

Wal. Indeed thou art, to love the man That spurns thee!

Julia. Love him! Love! If hate could find A word more harsh than its own name, I'd take it, To speak the love I bear him! [Weeps.]

Wal. Write thy own name, And show him how near akin thy hate's to hate.

Julia. [Writes.] 'Tis done!

Wal. 'Tis well! I'll come to you anon! [Goes out.]

Julia. [Alone.] I'm glad 'tis done! I'm very glad 'tis done! I've done the thing I ought. From my disgrace This lord shall lift me 'bove the reach of scorn - That idly wags its tongue, where wealth and state Need only beckon to have crowds to laud! Then how the tables change! The hand he spurned His betters take! Let me remember that! I'll grace my rank! I will! I'll carry it As I was born to it! I warrant none Shall say it fits me not:- but, one and all Confess I wear it bravely, as I ought! And he shall hear it! Ay, and he shall see it! I will roll by him in an equipage Would mortgage his estate - but he shall own His slight of me was my advancement! Love me! He never loved me! if he had, he ne'er Had given me up! Love's not a spider's web

But fit to mesh a fly - that you can break By only blowing on't! He never loved me! He knows not what love is! - or, if he does, He has not been o'erchary of his peace! And that he'll find when I'm another's wife, Lost! - lost to him for ever! Tears again! Why should I weep for him? Who make their woes. Deserve them! What have I to do with tears?

[Enter HELEN.]

Helen. News, Julia, news!

Julia. What! is't about Sir Thomas?

Helen. Sir Thomas, say you? He's no more Sir Thomas! That cousin lives, as heir to whom, his wealth And title came to him.

Julia. Was he not dead?

Helen. No more than I am dead.

Julia. I would 'twere not so.

Helen. What say you, Julia?

Julia. Nothing!

Helen. I could kiss That cousin! couldn't you, Julia?

Julia. Wherefore?

Helen. Why For coming back to life again, as 'twere Upon his cousin to revenge you.

Julia. Helen!

Helen. Indeed 'tis true. With what a sorry grace The gentleman will bear himself without His title! Master Clifford! Have you not Some token to return him? Some love-letter? Some brooch? Some pin? Some anything? I'll be Your messenger, for nothing but the pleasure Of calling him plain "Master Clifford."

Julia. Helen!

Helen. Or has he aught of thine? Write to him, Julia, Demanding it! Do, Julia, if you love me; And I'll direct it in a schoolboy's hand, As round as I can write, "To Master Clifford."

Julia. Helen!

Helen. I'll think of fifty thousand ways To mortify him! I've a twentieth cousin, A care-for-nought, at mischief. Him I'll set, With twenty other madcaps like himself, To walk the streets the traitor most frequents And give him salutation as he passes - "How do you, Master Clifford?"

Julia. [Highly incensed.] Helen!

Helen. Bless me!

Julia. I hate you, Helen!

[Enter MODUS.]

Mod. Joy for you, fair lady! Our baronet is now plain gentleman - And hardly that, not master of the means To bear himself as such. The kinsman lives Whose only rumoured death gave wealth to him, And title. A hard creditor he proves, Who keeps strict reckoning -

will have interest. As well as principal. A ruined man Is now Sir Thomas Clifford!

Helen. I'm glad on't.

Mod. And so am I, A scurvy trick it was He served you, madam. Use a lady so! I merely bore with him. I never liked him.

Helen. No more did I. No, never could I think He looked his title.

Mod. No, nor acted it. If rightly they report, he ne'er disbursed To entertain his friends, 'tis broadly said, A hundred pounds in the year! He was most poor In the appointments of a man of rank, Possessing wealth like his. His horses, hacks! His gentleman, a footman! and his footman, A groom! The sports that men of quality And spirit countenance, he kept aloof from, From scruple of economy, not taste, - As racing and the like. In brief, he lacked Those shining points that, more than name, denote High breeding; and, moreover, was a man Of very shallow learning.

Julia. Silence, sir! For shame!

Helen. Why, Julia!

Julia. Speak not to me! Poor! Most poor! I tell you, sir, he was the making Of fifty gentlemen - each one of whom Were more than peer for thee! His title, sir, Lent him no grace he did not pay it back! Though it had been the highest of the high, He would have looked it, felt it, acted it, As thou couldst ne'er have done! When found you out You liked him not? It was not ere to-day! Or that base spirit I must reckon yours

Which smiles where it would scowl - can stoop to hate And fear to show it! He was your better, sir, And is! - Ay, is! though stripped of rank and wealth, His nature's 'bove or fortune's love or spite, To blazon or to blurr it! [Retires.]

Mod. [To HELEN.] I was told Much to disparage him - I know not wherefore.

Helen. And so was I, and know as much the cause.

[Enter MASTER WALTER, with parchments.]

Wal. Joy, my Julia! Impatient love has foresight! Lo you here The marriage deeds filled up, except a blank To write your jointure. What you will, my girl! Is this a lover? Look! Three thousand pounds Per annum for your private charges! Ha! There's pin-money! Is this a lover? Mark What acres, forests, tenements, are taxed For your revenue; and so set apart, That finger cannot touch them, save thine own. Is this a lover? What good fortune's thine! Thou dost not speak; but, 'tis the way with joy! With richest heart, it has the poorest tongue!

Mod. What great good fortune's this you speak of, sir?

Wal. A coronet, Master Modus! You behold The wife elect, sir, of no less a man Than the new Earl of Rochdale - heir of him That's recently deceased.

Helen. My dearest Julia, Much joy to you!

Mod. All good attend you, madam!

Wal. This letter brings excuses from his lordship,

Whose absence it accounts for. He repairs To his estate in Lancashire, and thither We follow.

Julia. When, sir?

Wal. Now. This very hour.

Julia. This very hour! O cruel, fatal haste!

Wal. "O cruel, fatal haste!" What meanest thou? Have I done wrong to do thy bidding, then? I have done no more. Thou wast an offcast bride, And wouldst be an affianced one - thou art so! Thou'dst have the slight that marked thee out for scorn, Converted to a means of gracing thee - It is so! If our wishes come too soon, What can make sure of welcome? In my zeal To win thee thine, thou know'st, at any time I'd play the steed, whose will to serve his lord, With his last breath gives his last bound for him! Since only noon have I despatched what well Had kept a brace of clerks, and more, on foot - And then, perhaps, had been to do again! - Not finished sure, complete - the compact firm, As fate itself had sealed it!

Julia. Give you thanks! Though 'twere my death! my death!

Wal. Thy death! indeed, For happiness like this, one well might die! Take thy lord's letter! Well?

[Enter THOMAS, with a letter.]

Thos. This letter, sir, The gentleman that served Sir Thomas Clifford - Or him that was Sir Thomas - gave to me For Mistress Julia.

Julia. Give it me!

[Throwing away the one she holds.]

Wal. [Snatching it.] For what? Wouldst read it? He's a bankrupt! stripped of title, House, chattels, lands, and all! A naked bankrupt, With neither purse, nor trust! Wouldst read his letter? A beggar! Yea, a very beggar! - fasts, unless He dines on alms! How durst he send thee a letter! A fellow cut on this hand, and on that; Bows and is cut again, and bows again! Who pays you fifty smiles for half a one, - And that given grudgingly! To you a letter! I burst with choler! Thus I treat his letter!

[Tears and throws it on the ground.]

So! I was wrong to let him ruffle me; He is not worth the spending anger on! I prithee, Master Modus, use despatch, And presently make ready for our ride. You, Helen, to my Julia look - a change Of dresses will suffice. She must have new ones, Matches for her new state! Haste, friends. My Julia! Why stand you poring there upon the ground? Time flies. Your rise astounds you? Never heed - You'll play my lady countess like a queen!

[They go out.]

ACT IV.

SCENE I. - A Room in the Earl of Rochdale's

[Eater HELEN.]

Helen. I'm weary wandering from room to room; A castle after all is but a house - The dullest one when lacking company. Were I at home, I could be company Unto myself. I see not Master Walter, He's ever with his ward. I see not her. By Master Walter's will she bides alone. My father stops in town. I can't see him. My cousin makes his books his company. I'll go to bed and sleep. No - I'll stay up And plague my cousin into making love! For, that he loves me, shrewdly I suspect. How dull he is that hath not sense to see What lies before him, and he'd like to find! I'll change my treatment of him. Cross him, where Before I used to humour him. He comes, Poring upon a book. What's that you read?

[Enter MODUS.]

Mod. Latin, sweet cousin.

Helen. 'Tis a naughty tongue, I fear, and teaches men to lie.

Mod. To lie!

Helen. You study it. You call your cousin sweet, And treat her as you would a crab. As sour 'Twould seem you think her, as you covet her! Why how the monster stares, and looks about! You construe Latin, and can't construe that!

Mod. I never studied women.

Helen. No; nor men. Else would you better know their ways: nor read In presence of a lady. [Strikes the book from his hand.]

Mod. Right you say, And well you served me, cousin, so to strike The volume from my hand. I own my fault; So please you - may I pick it up again? I'll put it in my pocket!

Helen. Pick it up. He fears me as I were his grandmother! What is the book?

Mod. 'Tis Ovid's Art of Love.

Helen. That Ovid was a fool!

Mod. In what?

Helen. In that: To call that thing an art, which art is none.

Mod. And is not love an art?

Helen. Are you a fool, As well as Ovid? Love an art! No art But taketh time and pains to learn. Love comes With neither! Is't to hoard such grain as that, You went to college? Better stay at home, And study homely English.

Mod. Nay, you know not The argument.

Helen. I don't? I know it better Than ever Ovid did! The face - the form - The heart - the mind we fancy, cousin; that's The argument! Why, cousin, you know nothing. Suppose a lady were in love with thee: Couldst thou by Ovid, cousin, find it out? Couldst find it out, wast thou in love thyself? Could Ovid, cousin, teach thee to make love? I could, that never read him! You begin With melancholy; then to sadness; then To sickness; then to dying - but not die! She would not let thee, were she of my mind! She'd take compassion on thee. Then for hope; From hope to confidence; from confidence To boldness; - then you'd speak; at first entreat; Then urge; then flout; then argue; then enforce; Make prisoner of her hand; besiege her waist; Threaten her lips with storming; keep thy word And carry her! My sampler 'gainst thy Ovid! Why cousin, are you frightened, that you stand As you were stricken dumb? The case is clear, You are no soldier. You'll ne'er win a battle. You care too much for blows!

Mod. You wrong me there, At school I was the champion of my form; And since I went to college -

Helen. That for college!

Mod. Nay, hear me!

Helen. Well? What, since you went to college? You know what men are set down for, who boast Of their own bravery! Go on, brave cousin: What, since you went to college? Was there not One Quentin Halworth there? You know there was, And that he was your master!

Mod. He my master! Thrice was he worsted by me.

Helen. Still was he Your master.

Mod. He allowed I had the best! Allowed it, mark me! nor to me alone, But twenty I could name.

Helen. And mastered you At last! Confess it, cousin, 'tis the truth! A proctor's daughter you did both affect - Look at me and deny it! Of the twain She more affected you; - I've caught you now, Bold cousin! Mark you? opportunity On opportunity she gave you, sir - Deny it if you can! - but though to others, When you discoursed of her, you were a flame; To her you were a wick that would not light, Though held in the very fire! And so he won her - Won her, because he wooed her like a man. For all your cuffings, cuffing you again With most usurious interest. Now, sir, Protest that you are valiant!

Mod. Cousin Helen!

Helen. Well, sir?

Mod. The tale is all a forgery!

Helen. A forgery!

Mod. From first to last; ne'er spoke I To a proctor's daughter while I was at college.

Helen. 'Twas a scrivener's then - or somebody's. But what concerns it whose? Enough, you loved her! And, shame upon you, let another take her!

Mod. Cousin, I'll tell you, if you'll only hear me, I

loved no woman while I was at college - Save one, and her I fancied ere I went there.

Helen. Indeed! Now I'll retreat, if he's advancing. Comes he not on! O what a stock's the man! Well, cousin?

Mod. Well! What more wouldst have me say? I think I've said enough.

Helen. And so think I. I did but jest with you. You are not angry? Shake hands! Why, cousin, do you squeeze me so?

Mod. [Letting her go.] I swear I squeezed you not.

Helen. You did not?

Mod. No. I'll die if I did!

Helen. Why then you did not, cousin, So let's shake hands again - [He takes her hand as before.] O go and now Read Ovid! Cousin, will you tell me one thing: Wore lovers ruffs in Master Ovid's time? Behoved him teach them, then, to put them on; - And that you have to learn. Hold up your head! Why, cousin, how you blush! Plague on the ruff! I cannot give't a set. You're blushing still! Why do you blush, dear cousin? So! - 'twill beat me! I'll give it up.

Mod. Nay, prithee, don't - try on!

Helen. And if I do, I fear you'll think me bold.

Mod. For what?

Helen. To trust my face so near to thine.

Mod. I know not what you mean.

Helen. I'm glad you don't! Cousin, I own right well behaved you are, Most marvellously well behaved! They've bred You well at college. With another man My lips would be in danger! Hang the ruff!

Mod. Nay, give it up, nor plague thyself, dear cousin.

Helen. Dear fool! [Throws the ruff on the ground.] I swear the ruff is good for just As little as its master! There! - 'Tis spoiled - You'll have to get another! Hie for it, And wear it in the fashion of a wisp, Ere I adjust it for thee! Farewell, cousin! You'd need to study Ovid's Art of Love.

[HELEN goes out.]

Mod. [Solus.] Went she in anger! I will follow her, - No, I will not! Heigho! I love my cousin! O would that she loved me! Why did she taunt me With backwardness in love? What could she mean? Sees she I love her, and so laughs at me, Because I lack the front to woo her? Nay, I'll woo her then! Her lips shall be in danger, When next she trusts them near me! Looked she at me To-day as never did she look before! A bold heart, Master Modus! 'Tis a saying A faint one never won fair lady yet! I'll woo my cousin, come what will on't. Yes:

[Begins reading again, throws down the book.]

Hang Ovid's Art of Love! I'll woo my cousin!
[Goes out.]

SCENE II. - The Banqueting-room in the Earl of Rochdale's Mansion.

[Enter MASTER WALTER and JULIA.]

Wal. This is the banqueting-room. Thou seest as far It leaves the last behind, as that excels The former ones. All is proportion here And harmony! Observe! The massy pillars May well look proud to bear the gilded dome. You mark those full-length portraits? They're the heads, The stately heads, of his ancestral line. Here o'er the feast they haply still preside! Mark those medallions! Stand they forth or not In bold and fair relief? Is not this brave?

Julia. [Abstractedly.] It is.

Wal. It should be so. To cheer the blood That flows in noble veins is made the feast That gladdens here! You see this drapery? 'Tis richest velvet! Fringe and tassels, gold! Is not this costly?

Julia. Yes.

Wal. And chaste, the while? Both chaste and costly?

Julia. Yes.

Wal. Come hither! There's a mirror for you. See!

One sheet from floor to ceiling! Look into it, Salute its mistress! Dost not know her?

Julia. [Sighing deeply.] Yes.

Wal. And sighest thou to know her? Wait until To-morrow, when the banquet shall be spread In the fair hall; the guests - already bid, Around it; here, her lord; and there, herself; Presiding o'er the cheer that hails him bridegroom, And her the happy bride! Dost hear me?

Julia. [Sighing still more deeply.] Yes.

Wal. These are the day-rooms only, we have seen. For public and domestic uses kept. I'll show you now the lodging-rooms.

[Goes, then turns and observes JULIA standing perfectly abstracted.]

You're tired. Let it be till after dinner, then. Yet one I'd like thee much to see - the bridal chamber.

[JULIA starts, crosses her hands upon her breast, and looks upwards.]

I see you're tired: yet it is worth the viewing, If only for the tapestry which shows The needle like the pencil glows with life;

[Brings down chairs - they sit.]

The story's of a page who loved the dame He served - a princess! - Love's a heedless thing! That never takes account of obstacles; Makes plains of mountains, rivulets of seas, That part it from its wish. So proved the page, Who from a state so lowly, looked so high, - But love's a greater lackwit still than this. Say it aspires - that's gain! Love stoops - that's loss! You know what comes. The princess loved the page. Shall I go on, or here leave off?

Julia. Go on.

Wal. Each side of the chamber shows a different stage Of this fond page, and fonder lady's love. {2} First - no, it is not that.

Julia. Oh, recollect!

Wal. And yet it is.

Julia. No doubt it is. What is 't?

Wal. He holds to her a salver, with a cup; His cheeks more mantling with his passion than The cup with the ruby wine. She heeds him not, For too great heed of him:- but seems to hold Debate betwixt her passion and her pride - That's like to lose the day. You read it in Her vacant eye, knit brow, and parted lips, Which speak a heart too busy all within To note what's done without. Like you the tale?

Julia. I list to every word.

Wal. The next side paints The page upon his knee. He has told his tale; And found that when he lost his heart, he played No losing game: but won a richer one! There may you read in him, how love would seem Most humble when most bold, - you question which Appears to kiss her hand - his breath, or lips! In her you read how wholly lost is she Who trusts her heart to love. Shall I give o'er?

Julia. Nay, tell it to the end. Is't melancholy?

Wal. To answer that, would mar the story.

Julia. Right.

Wal. The third side now we come to.

Julia. What shows that?

Wal. The page and princess still. But stands her sire Between them. Stern he grasps his daughter's arm, Whose eyes like fountains play; while through her tears Her passion shines, as through the fountain drops The sun! His minions crowd around the page! They drag him to a dungeon.

Julia. Hapless youth!

Wal. Hapless indeed, that's twice a captive! heart And body both in bonds. But that's the chain, Which balance cannot weigh, rule measure, touch Define the texture of, or eye detect, That's forged by the subtle craft of love! No need to tell you that he wears it. Such The cunning of the hand that plied the loom, You've but to mark the straining of his eye, To feel the coil yourself!

Julia. I feel't without! You've finished with the third side; now the fourth!

Wal. It brings us to a dungeon, then.

Julia. The page, The thrall of love, more than the dungeon's thrall, Is there?

Wal. He is. He lies in fetters.

Julia. Hard! Hard as the steel, the hands that put them on.

Wal. Some one unrivets them!

Julia. The princess? 'Tis!

Wal. It is another page.

Julia. It is herself!

Wal. Her skin is fair; and his is berry-brown. His locks are raven black; and hers are gold.

Julia. Love's cunning of disguises! spite of locks, Skin, vesture, - it is she, and only she What will not constant woman do for love That's loved with constancy! Set her the task, Virtue approving, that will baffle her! O'ertax her stooping, patience, courage, wit! My life upon it, 'tis the princess' self, Transformed into a page!

Wal. The dungeon door Stands open, and you see beyond -

Julia. Her father!

Wal. No; a steed.

Julia. [Starting up.] O, welcome steed, My heart bounds at the thought of thee! Thou comest To bear the page from bonds to liberty. What else?

Wal. [Rising.] The story's told.

Julia. Too briefly told; O happy princess, that had wealth and state To lay them down for love! Whose constant love Appearances approved, not falsified! A winner in thy loss, as well as gain.

Wal. Weighs love so much?

Julia. What would you weigh 'gainst love That's true? Tell me with what you'd turn the scale? Yea, make the index waver? Wealth? A feather! Rank? Tinsel against bullion in the balance! The love of kindred? That to set 'gainst love! Friendship comes nearest to't; but put it in, Friendship will kick the beam! - weigh nothing 'gainst it! Weigh love against the world! Yet are they happy that have naught to say to it.

Wal. And such a one art thou. Who wisely wed, Wed happily. The love thou speak'st of, A flower is only, that its season has, Which they must look to see the withering of, Who pleasure in its budding and its bloom! But wisdom is the constant evergreen Which lives the whole year through! Be that, your flower!

[Enter a Servant.]

Well?

Serv. My lord's secretary is without. He brings a letter for her ladyship, And craves admittance to her.

Wal. Show him in.

Julia. No.

Wal. Thou must see him. To show slight to him, Were slighting him that sent him. Show him in!

[Servant goes out.]

Some errand proper for thy private ear, Besides the letter he may bring. What mean This paleness and this trembling? Mark me, Julia! If, from these nuptials, which thyself invited - Which at thy seeking came - thou wouldst be freed, Thou hast gone too far! Receding were disgrace, Sooner than see thee suffer which, the hearts That love thee most would wish thee dead! Reflect! Take thought! collect thyself! With dignity Receive thy bridegroom's messenger! for sure As dawns to-morrow's sun, to-morrow night Sees thee a wedded bride!

[Goes out.]

Julia. [Alone.] A wedded bride! Is it a dream? Is it a phantasm? 'Tis Too horrible for reality! for aught else Too palpable! O would it were a dream! How would I bless the sun that waked me from it! I perish! Like some desperate mariner Impatient of a strange and hostile land, Who rashly hoists his sail and puts to sea, And being fast on reefs and quicksands borne, Essays in vain once more to make the land, Whence wind and current drive him; I'm wrecked By mine own act! What! no escape? no hope? None! I must e'en abide these hated nuptials! Hated! - Ah! own it, and then curse thyself! That madest the bane thou loathest - for the love Thou bear'st to one who never can be thine! Yes - love! Deceive thyself no longer. False To say 'tis pity for his fall - respect, Engendered by a hollow world's disdain, Which hoots whom fickle fortune cheers no more! 'Tis none of these; 'tis love - and if not love, Why then idolatry! Ay, that's the name To speak the broadest, deepest, strongest passion, That ever woman's heart was borne away by! He comes! Thou'dst play the lady, - play it now!

[Enter a Servant, conducting CLIFFORD, plainly attired as the EARL OF ROCHDALE'S Secretary.]

Servant. His lordship's secretary.

[Servant goes out.]

Julia. Speaks he not? Or does he wait for orders to unfold His business? Stopped his business till I spoke, I'd hold my peace for ever!

[CLIFFORD kneels; presenting a letter.]

Does he kneel? A lady am I to my heart's content! Could he unmake me that which claims his knee, I'd kneel to him - I would! I would! - Your will?

Clif. This letter from my lord.

Julia. O fate! Who speaks?

Clif. The secretary of my lord.

Julia. I breathe! I could have sworn 'twas he!

[Makes an effort to look at him, but is unable.]

So like the voice - I dare not look, lest there the form should stand! How came he by that voice? 'Tis

Clifford's voice, If ever Clifford spoke! My fears come back - Clifford the secretary of my lord! Fortune hath freaks, but none so mad as that! It cannot be! - It should not be! - A look, And all were set at rest.

[Tries to look at him again, but cannot.]

So strong my fears, Dread to confirm them takes away the power To try and end them! Come the worst, I'll look.

[She tries again; and again is unequal to the task.]

I'd sink before him if I met his eye!

Clif. Will't please your ladyship to take the letter?
Julia. There Clifford speaks again! Not Clifford's heart Could more make Clifford's voice! Not Clifford's tongue And lips more frame it into Clifford's speech! A question, and 'tis over! Know I you?

Clif. Reverse of fortune, lady, changes friends; It turns them into strangers. What I am I have not always been!

Julia. Could I not name you?

Clif. If your disdain for one, perhaps too bold When hollow fortune called him favourite, - Now by her fickleness perforce reduced To take an humble tone, would suffer you -

Julia. I might?

Clif. You might!

Julia. Oh, Clifford! is it you?

Clif. Your answer to my lord.

[Gives the letter.]

Julia. Your lord!

[Mechanically taking it.]

Clif. Wilt write it? Or, will it please you send a verbal one? I'll bear it faithfully.

Julia. You'll bear it?

Clif. Madam, Your pardon, but my haste is somewhat urgent. My lord's impatient, and to use despatch Were his repeated orders.

Julia. Orders? Well, I'll read the letter, sir. 'Tis right you mind His lordship's orders. They are paramount! Nothing should supersede them! - stand beside them! They merit all your care, and have it! Fit, Most fit, they should! Give me the letter, sir.

Clif. You have it, madam.

Julia. So! How poor a thing I look! so lost, while he is all himself! Have I no pride?

[She rings, the Servant enters.]

Paper, and pen, and ink! If he can freeze, 'tis time that I grow cold! I'll read the letter.

[Opens it, and holds it as about to read it.]

Mind his orders! So! Quickly he fits his habits to his fortunes! He serves my lord with all his will! His heart's In his vocation. So! Is this the letter? 'Tis upside down - and here I'm poring on't! Most fit I let him see me play the fool! Shame! Let me be myself!

[A Servant enters with materials for writing.]

A table, sir, And chair.

[The Servant brings a table and chair, and goes out. She sits a while, vacantly gazing on the letter - then looks at CLIFFORD.]

How plainly shows his humble suit! It fits not him that wears it! I have wronged him! He can't be happy - does not look it! - is not. That eye which reads the ground is argument Enough! He loves me. There I let him stand, And I am sitting!

[Rises, takes a chair, and approaches CLIFFORD.]

Pray you take a chair.

[He bows, as acknowledging and declining the honour. She looks at him a while.]

Clifford, why don't you speak to me?

[She weeps.]

Clif. I trust You're happy.

Julia. Happy! Very, very happy! You see I weep, I am so happy! Tears Are signs, you know, of naught but happiness! When first I saw you, little did I look To be so happy! - Clifford!

Clif. Madam?

Julia. Madam! I call thee Clifford, and thou call'st me madam!

Clif. Such the address my duty stints me to. Thou art the wife elect of a proud Earl, Whose humble secretary, sole, am I.

Julia. Most right! I had forgot! I thank you, sir, For so reminding me; and give you joy, That what, I see, had been a burthen to you, Is fairly off your hands.

Clif. A burthen to me! Mean you yourself? Are you that burthen, Julia? Say that the sun's a burthen to the earth! Say that the blood's a burthen to the heart! Say health's a burthen, peace, contentment, joy, Fame, riches, honours! everything that man Desires, and gives the name of blessing to E'en such a burthen, Julia were to me, Had fortune let me wear her.

Julia. [Aside.] On the brink Of what a precipice I'm standing! Back, Back! while the faculty remains to do't! A minute longer, not the whirlpool's self More sure to suck me down! One effort! There!

[She returns to her seat, recovers her self-possession, takes up the letter, and reads.]

To wed to-morrow night! Wed whom? A man Whom I can never love! I should before Have thought of that. To-morrow night! This hour To-morrow! How I tremble! Happy bands To which my heart such freezing welcome gives, As sends an ague through me!

At what means Will not the desperate snatch! What's honour's price? Nor friends, nor lovers, - no, nor life itself! Clifford! This moment leave me!

[CLIFFORD retires up the stage out of JULIA'S sight.]

Is he gone? O docile lover! Do his mistress' wish That went against his own! Do it so soon Ere well 'twas uttered! No good-bye to her! No word! no look! 'Twas best that he so went! Alas, the strait of her, who owns that best, Which last she'd wish were done? What's left me now? To weep! To weep!

[Leans her head upon her arm, which rests upon the desk, - her other arm hanging listlessly at her side. CLIFFORD comes down the stage, looks a moment at her, approaches her, and kneeling, takes her hand.]

Clif. My Julia!

Julia. Here again! Up! up! By all thy hopes of Heaven, go hence! To stay's perdition to me! Look you, Clifford! Were there a grave where thou art kneeling now, I'd walk into 't, and be inearthed alive, Ere taint should touch my name! Should some one come And see thee kneeling thus! Let go my hand! Remember, Clifford, I'm a promised bride - And take thy arm away! It has no right To clasp my waist! Judge you so poorly of me, As think I'll suffer this? My honour, sir!

[She breaks from him, quitting her seat.]

I'm glad you've forced me to respect myself - You'll find that I can do so!

Clif. I was bold - Forgetful of your station and my own; There was a time I held your hand unchid! There was a time I might have clasped your waist - I had forgot that time was past and gone! I pray you, pardon me!

Julia. [Softened.] I do so, Clifford.

Clif. I shall no more offend.

Julia. Make sure of that. No longer is it fit thou keep'st thy post In's lordship's household. Give it up! A day - An hour remain not in it!

Clif. Wherefore?

Julia. Live In the same house with me, and I another's? Put miles, put leagues between us! The same land Should not contain us. Oceans should divide us - With barriers of constant tempests – such As mariners durst not tempt! O Clifford! Rash was the act so light that gave me up, That stung a woman's pride, and drove her mad - Till in her frenzy she destroyed her peace! Oh, it was rashly done! Had you reproved - Expostulated, - had you reasoned with me - Tried to find out what was indeed my heart, - I would have shown it - you'd have seen it. All Had been as naught can ever be again!

Clif. Lovest thou me, Julia?

Julia. Dost thou ask me, Clifford?

Clif. These nuptials may be shunned! -

Julia. With honour?

Clif. Yes!

Julia. Then take me! - Stop - hear me, and take me then! Let not thy passion be my counsellor! Deal with me, Clifford, as my brother. Be The jealous guardian of my spotless name! Scan thou my cause as 'twere thy sister's. Let Thy scrutiny o'erlook no point of it, - Nor turn it over once, but many a time:- That flaw, speck - yea, - the shade of one, - a soil So slight, not one out of a thousand eyes Could find it out, may not escape thee; then Say if these nuptials can be shunned with honour!

Clif. They can.

Julia. Then take me, Clifford! [They embrace.]

Wal. [Entering.] Ha! What's this? Ha! treason! What! my baronet that was, My secretary now? Your servant, sir! Is't thus you do the pleasure of your lord, - That for your service feeds you, clothes you, pays you! Or takest thou but the name of his dependent? What's here? - a letter. Fifty crowns to one A forgery! I'm wrong. It is his hand. This proves thee double traitor!

Clif. Traitor!

Julia. Nay, Control thy wrath, good Master Walter! Do - And I'll persuade him to go hence -

[MASTER WALTER retires up the stage.] I see For me thou bearest this, and thank thee, Clifford! As thou hast truly shown thy heart to me, So truly I to thee have opened mine! Time flies! To-morrow! If thy love can find A way, such as thou saidst, for my enlargement By any means thou canst, apprise me of it; And, soon as shown, I'll take it.

Wal. Is he gone?

Julia. He is this moment. If thou covetest me, Win me, and wear me! May I trust thee? Oh! If that's thy soul, that's looking through thine eyes, Thou lovest me, and I may! - I sicken, lest I never see thee more

Clif. As life is mine, The ring that on thy wedding-finger goes No hand but mine shall place there!

Wal. Lingers he?

Julia. For my sake, now away! And yet a word. By all thy hopes most dear, be true to me! Go now! - yet stay! Clifford, while you are here, I'm like a bark distressed and compassless, That by a beacon steers; when you're away, That bark alone and tossing miles at sea! Now go! Farewell! My compass - beacon - land! When shall my eyes be blessed with thee again!

Clif. Farewell! [Goes out.]

Julia. Art gone? All's chance - all's care - all's darkness.

[Is led off by MASTER WALTER.]

ACT V.

SCENE I. - An Apartment in the Earl of Rochdale's.

[Enter HELEN and FATHOM.]

Fath. The long and short of it is this - if she marries this lord, she'll break her heart! I wish you could see her, madam. Poor lady!

Helen. How looks she, prithee?

Fath. Marry, for all the world like a dripping-wet cambric handkerchief! She has no colour nor strength in her; and does nothing but weep - poor lady!

Helen. Tell me again what said she to thee?

Fath. She offered me all she was mistress of to take the letter to Master Clifford. She drew her purse from her pocket - the ring from her finger - she took her very earrings out of her ears - but I was forbidden, and refused. And now I'm sorry for it! Poor lady!

Helen. Thou shouldst be sorry. Thou hast a hard heart, Fathom.

Fath. I, madam! My heart is as soft as a woman's. You should have seen me when I came out of her chamber - poor lady!

Helen. Did you cry?

Fath. No; but I was as near it as possible. I a hard heart! I would do anything to serve her, poor sweet lady!

Helen. Will you take her letter, asks she you again?

Fath. No - I am forbid.

Helen. Will you help Master Clifford to an interview with her?

Fath. No - Master Walter would find it out.

Helen. Will you contrive to get me into her chamber?

Fath. No - you would be sure to bring me into mischief.

Helen. Go to! You would do nothing to serve her. You a soft heart! You have no heart at all! You feel not for her!

Fath. But I tell you I do - and good right I have to feel for her. I have been in love myself.

Helen. With your dinner!

Fath. I would it had been! My pain would soon have been over, and at little cost. A fortune I squandered upon her! - trinkets - trimmings - treatings - what swallowed up the revenue of a whole year! Wasn't I in love? Six months I courted her, and a dozen crowns all but one did I disburse for her in that time! Wasn't I in love? An hostler - a tapster - and a constable, courted her at the same time, and I offered to cudgel the whole three of them for her! Wasn't I in love?

Helen. You are a valiant man, Fathom.

Fath. Am not I? Walks not the earth the man I am afraid of.

Helen. Fear you not Master Walter?

Fath. No.

Helen. You do!

Fath. I don't!

Helen. I'll prove it to you. You see him breaking your young mistress's heart, and have not the manhood to stand by her.

Fath. What could I do for her?

Helen. Let her out of prison. It were the act of a man.

Fath. That man am I!

Helen. Well said, brave Fathom!

Fath. But my place!

Helen. I'll provide thee with a better one.

Fath. 'Tis a capital place! So little to do, and so much to get for't. Six pounds in the year; two suits of livery;

shoes and stockings, and a famous larder. He'd be a bold man that would put such a place in jeopardy. My place, madam, my place!

Helen. I tell thee I'll provide thee with a better place. Thou shalt have less to do, and more to get. Now, Fathom, hast thou courage to stand by thy mistress?

Fath. I have!

Helen. That's right.

Fath. I'll let my lady out.

[Enter MASTER WALTER unperceived.]

Helen. That's right. When, Fathom?

Fath. To-night.

Helen. She is to be married to-night.

Fath. This evening, then. Master Walter is now in the library, the key is on the outside, and I'll lock him in.

Helen. Excellent! You'll do it?

Fath. Rely upon it. How he'll stare when he finds himself a prisoner, and my young lady at liberty!

Helen. Most excellent! You'll be sure to do it?

Fath. Depend upon me! When Fathom undertakes a thing, he defies fire and water -

Wal. [Coming forward.] Fathom!

Fath. Sir!

Wal. Assemble straight the servants.

Fath. Yes, sir!

Wal. Mind, And have them in the hall when I come down.

Fath. Yes, sir!

Wal. And see you do not stir a step, But where I order you.

Fath. Not an inch, sir!

Wal. See that you don't - away! So, my fair mistress,

[FATHOM goes out.]

What's this you have been plotting? An escape For mistress Julia?

Helen. I avow it.

Wal. Do you?

Helen. Yes; and moreover to your face I tell you, Most hardly do you use her!

Wal. Verily!

Helen. I wonder where's her spirit! Had she mine She would not take 't so easily. Do you mean To force this marriage on her?

Wal. With your leave.

Helen. You laugh.

Wal. Without it, then. I don't laugh now.

Helen. If I were she, I'd find a way to escape.

Wal. What would you do?

Helen. I'd leap out of the window!

Wal. Your window should be barred.

Helen. I'd cheat you still! - I'd hang myself ere I'd be forced to marry!

Wal. Well said! You shall be married, then, tonight.

Helen. Married to-night!

Wal. As sure as I have said it.

Helen. Two words to that. Pray who's to be my bridegroom?

Wal. A daughter's husband is her father's choice.

Helen. My father's daughter ne'er shall wed such husband!

Wal. Indeed!

Helen. I'll pick a husband for myself.

Wal. Indeed!

Helen. Indeed, sir; and indeed again!

Wal. Go dress you for the marriage ceremony.

Helen. But, Master Walter, what is it you mean?

[Enter MODUS.]

Wal. Here comes your cousin; - he shall be your bridesman! The thought's a sudden one, - that will excuse Defect in your appointments. A plain dress, - So 'tis of white, - will do.

Helen. I'll dress in black. I'll quit the castle.

Wal. That you shall not do. Its doors are guarded by my lord's domestics, Its avenues - its grounds. What you must do, Do with a good grace! In an hour, or less, Your father will be here. Make up your mind To take with thankfulness the man he gives you. Now, [Aside] if they find not out how beat their hearts, I have no skill, not I, in feeling pulses.

[Goes out.]

Helen. Why, cousin Modus! What! will you stand by And see me forced to marry? Cousin Modus! Have you not got a tongue? Have you not eyes? Do you not see I'm very - very ill, And not a chair in all the corridor?

Mod. I'll find one in the study.

Helen. Hang the study!

Mod. My room's at hand. I'll fetch one thence.

Helen. You shan't I'd faint ere you came back!

Mod. What shall I do?

Helen. Why don't you offer to support me? Well? Give me your arm - be quick! [MODUS offers his arm.] Is that the way To help a lady when she's like to faint? I'll drop unless you catch me! [MODUS supports her.] That will do. I'm better now - [MODUS offers to leave her] don't leave me! Is one well Because one's better? Hold my hand. Keep so. I'll soon recover so you move not. Loves he -

[Aside.]

Which I'll be sworn he does, he'll own it now. Well, cousin Modus?

Mod. Well, sweet cousin!

Helen. Well? You heard what Master Walter said?

Mod. I did.

Helen. And would you have me marry? Can't you speak? Say yes or no.

Mod. No, cousin!

Helen. Bravely said! And why, my gallant cousin?

Mod. Why?

Helen. Ay, why? - Women, you know, are fond of reasons - why Would you not have me marry? How you blush! Is it because you do not know the reason?

You mind me of a story of a cousin Who once her cousin such a question asked. He had not been to college, though - for books, Had passed his time in reading ladies' eyes. Which he could construe marvellously well, Though writ in language all symbolical. Thus stood they once together, on a day - As we stand now - discoursed as we discourse, - But with this difference, - fifty gentle words He spoke to her, for one she spoke to him! - What a dear cousin! Well, as I did say, As now I questioned thee, she questioned him. And what was his reply? To think of it Sets my heart beating - 'twas so kind a one! So like a cousin's answer - a dear cousin! A gentle, honest, gallant, loving cousin! What did he say? - A man might find it out, Though never read he Ovid's Art of Love - What did he say? He'd marry her himself! How stupid are you, cousin! Let me go!

Mod. You are not well yet?

Helen. Yes.

Mod. I'm sure you're not.

Helen. I'm sure I am.

Mod. Nay, let me hold you, cousin! I like it.

Helen. Do you? I would wager you You could not tell me why you like it. Well? You see how true I know you! How you stare! What see you in my face to wonder at?

Mod. A pair of eyes!

Helen. At last he'll find his tongue - [Aside.] And saw

you ne'er a pair of eyes before?

Mod. Not such a pair.

Helen. And why?

Mod. They are so bright! You have a Grecian nose.

Helen. Indeed.

Mod. Indeed!

Helen. What kind of mouth have I?

Mod. A handsome one. I never saw so sweet a pair of lips! I ne'er saw lips at all till now, dear cousin!

Helen. Cousin, I'm well, - you need not hold me now. Do you not hear? I tell you I am well! I need your arm no longer - take 't away! So tight it locks me, 'tis with pain I breathe! Let me go, cousin! Wherefore do you hold Your face so close to mine? What do you mean?

Mod. You've questioned me, and now I'll question you.

Helen. What would you learn?

Mod. The use of lips.

Helen. To speak.

Mod. Naught else?

Helen. How bold my modest cousin grows! Why, other use know you?

Mod. I do!

Helen. Indeed! You're wondrous wise? And pray what is it?

Mod. This! [Attempts to kiss her.]

Helen. Soft! my hand thanks you, cousin - for my lips I keep them for a husband! - Nay, stand off! I'll not be held in manacles again! Why do you follow me?

Mod. I love you, cousin!

Helen. O cousin, say you so! That's passing strange! Falls out most crossly - is a dire mishap - A thing to sigh for, weep for, languish for, And die for!

Mod. Die for!

Helen, Yes, with laughter, cousin, For, cousin, I love you!

Mod. And you'll be mine?

Helen. I will.

Mod. Your hand upon it.

Helen. Hand and heart. Hie to thy dressing-room, and I'll to mine - Attire thee for the altar - so will I. Whoe'er may claim me, thou'rt the man shall have me. Away! Despatch! But hark you, ere you go, Ne'er brag of reading Ovid's Art of Love!

Mod. And cousin! stop - one little word with you!

[She returns, he snatches a kiss - They go out severally.]

SCENE II. - Julia's Chamber.

[Enter JULIA.]

Julia. No word from him, and evening now set in! He cannot play me false! His messenger Is dogged - or letter intercepted. I'm Beset with spies! - No rescue! - No escape! - The hour at hand that brings my bridegroom home! No relative to aid me! friend to counsel me.

[A knock at the door.]

Come in.

[Enter two Female Attendants.]

Your will?

First Attendant. Your toilet waits, my lady; 'Tis time you dress.

Julia. 'Tis time I die! [A peal of bells.] What's that?

First Attendant. Your wedding bells, my lady.

Julia. Merrily They ring my knell! [Second Attendant presents an open case.] And pray you what are these?

Second Attendant. Your wedding jewels.

Julia. Set them by.

Second Attendant. Indeed. Was ne'er a braver set! A necklace, brooch, And earrings all of brilliants, with a hoop To guard your wedding ring.

Julia. 'Twould need a guard That lacks a heart to keep it!

Second Attendant. Here's a heart Suspended from the necklace - one huge diamond Imbedded in a host of smaller ones! Oh! how it sparkles!

Julia. Show it me! Bright heart, Thy lustre, should I wear thee, will be false, - For thou the emblem art of love and truth, - From her that wears thee unto him that gives thee. Back to thy case! Better thou ne'er shouldst leave it - Better thy gems a thousand fathoms deep In their native mine again, than grace my neck, And lend thy fair face to palm off a lie!

First Attendant. Will't please you dress?

Julia. Ah! in infected clothes New from a pest-house! Leave me! If I dress, I dress alone! O for a friend! Time gallops!

[Attendants go out.]

He that should guard me is mine enemy! Constrains me to abide the fatal die, My rashness, not my reason cast! He comes, That will exact the forfeit! - Must I pay it? - E'en at the cost of utter bankruptcy! What's to be done? Pronounce the vow that parts My body from my soul! To what it loathes Links that, while this is linked to what it loves! Condemned to such perdition! What's to be done? Stand at the altar in an hour from this! An hour thence seated at his board - a wife Thence! - frenzy's in the thought! What's to be done?

[Enter MASTER WALTER.]

Wal. What! run the waves so high? Not ready yet! Your lord will soon be here! The guests collect.

Julia. Show me some way to 'scape these nuptials! Do it! Some opening for avoidance or escape, - Or to thy charge I'll lay a broken heart! It may be, broken vows, and blasted honour, Or else a mind distraught!

Wal. What's this?

Julia. The strait I'm fallen into my patience cannot bear. It frights my reason - warps my sense of virtue! Religion! - changes me into a thing I look at with abhorring!

Wal. Listen to me.

Julia. Listen to me! If this contract Thou holdest me to - abide thou the result! Answer to heaven for what I suffer! - act! Prepare thyself for such calamity To fall on me, and those whose evil stars Have linked them with me, as no past mishap, However rare, and marvellously sad Can parallel! lay thy account to live A smileless life, die an unpitied death - Abhorred, abandoned of thy kind, - as one Who had the guarding of a young maid's peace, - Looked on and saw her rashly peril it; And when she saw her danger, and confessed Her fault, compelled her to complete her ruin!

Wal. Hast done?

Julia. Another moment, and I have. Be warned! Beware how you abandon me To myself! I'm young, rash, inexperienced! tempted By most insufferable misery! Bold, desperate, and reckless! Thou hast age Experience, wisdom, and collectedness, - Power, freedom, - everything that I have not, Yet want, as none e'er wanted! Thou canst save me, Thou oughtst! thou must! I tell thee at his feet I'll fall a corse - ere mount his bridal bed! So choose betwixt my rescue and my grave; - And quickly too! The hour of sacrifice Is near! Anon the immolating priest Will summon me! Devise some speedy means To cheat the altar of its victim. Do it! Nor leave the task to me!

Wal. Hast done?

Julia. I have.

Wal. Then list to me - and silently, if not With patience. - [Brings chairs for himself and her.] How I watched thee from thy childhood I'll not recall to thee. Thy father's wisdom - Whose humble instrument I was - directed Your nonage should be passed in privacy, From your apt mind that far outstripped your years, Fearing the taint of an infected world; - For, in the rich grounds, weeds once taking root, Grow strong as flowers. He might be right or wrong! I thought him right; and therefore did his bidding. Most certainly he loved you - so did I; Ay! well as I had been myself your father!

[His hand is resting upon his knee, JULIA attempts to take it – he withdraws it - looks at her - she hangs her head.]

Well; you may take my hand! I need not say How fast you grew in knowledge, and in goodness, - That hope could scarce enjoy its golden dreams So soon fulfilment realised them all! Enough. You came to womanhood. Your heart, Pure as the leaf of the consummate bud, That's new unfolded by the smiling sun, And ne'er knew blight nor canker!

[JULIA attempts to place her other hand on his shoulder - he leans from her - looks at her - she hangs her head again.]

Put it there! Where left I off? I know! When a good woman Is fitly mated, she grows doubly good, How good soe'er before! I found the man I thought a match for thee; and, soon as found, Proposed him to thee. 'Twas your father's will, Occasion offering, you should be married Soon as you reached to womanhood. - You liked My choice, accepted him. - We came to town; Where, by important matter summoned thence, I left you an affianced bride!

Julia. You did! You did! [Leans her head upon her hand and weeps.]

Wal. Nay, check thy tears! Let judgment now, Not passion, be awake. On my return, I found thee - what? I'll not describe the thing I found thee then! I'll not describe my pangs To see thee such a thing! The engineer Who lays the last stone of his sea-built tower, It cost him years and years of toil to raise - And, smiling at it, tells the winds and waves To roar and whistle now - but, in a night, Beholds the tempest sporting in its place - May look aghast, as I did!

Julia. [Falling on her knees.] Pardon me! Forgive me! pity me!

Wal. Resume thy seat. [Raises her.] I pity thee; perhaps not thee alone It fits to sue for pardon.

Julia. Me alone! None other!

Wal. But to vindicate myself, I name thy lover's stern desertion of thee. What wast thou then with wounded pride? A thing To leap into a torrent! throw itself From a precipice! rush into a fire! I saw Thy madness - knew to thwart it were to chafe it - And humoured it to take that course, I thought, Adopted, least 'twould rue!

Julia. 'Twas wisely done.

Wal. At least 'twas for the best.

Julia. To blame thee for it Was adding shame to shame! But Master Walter, These nuptials! - must they needs go on?

Servant. [Entering.] More guests Arrive.

Wal. Attend to them. [Servant goes out.]

Julia. Dear Master Walter! Is there no way to escape these nuptials?

Wal. Know'st not What with these nuptials comes? Hast thou forgot?

Julia. What?

Wal. Nothing! - I did tell thee of a thing.

Julia. What was it?

Wal. To forget it was a fault! Look back and think.

Julia. I can't remember it.

Wal. Fathers, make straws your children! Nature's nothing, Blood nothing! Once in other veins it runs, It no more yearneth for the parent flood, Than doth the stream that from the source disparts. Talk not of love instinctive - what you call so Is but the brat of custom! Your own flesh By habit cleaves to you - without, Hath no adhesion. [Aside.] So; you have forgot You have a father, and are here to meet him!

Julia. I'll not deny it.

Wal. You should blush for't.

Julia. No! No! no: hear, Master Walter! what's a father That you've not been to me? Nay, turn not from me, For at the name a holy awe I own, That now almost inclines my knee to earth! But thou to me, except a father's name, Hast all the father been: the care - the love - The guidance - the protection of a father. Canst wonder, then, if like thy child I feel, - And feeling so, that father's claim forget Whom ne'er I knew save by the name of one? Oh, turn to me, and do not chide me! or If thou wilt chide, chide on! but turn to me!

Wal. [Struggling with emotion.] My Julia! [Embraces her.]

Julia. Now, dear Master Walter, hear me! Is there no way to 'scape these nuptials?

Wal. Julia, A promise made admits not of release, Save by consent or forfeiture of those Who hold it - so it should be pondered well Before we let it go. Ere man should say I broke the word I had the power to keep, I'd lose the life I had the power to part with! Remember, Julia, thou and I to-day Must, to thy father, of thy training render A strict account. While honour's left to us, We have something - nothing, having all but that. Now for thy last act of obedience, Julia! Present thyself before thy bridegroom! [She assents.] Good! My Julia's now herself! Show him thy heart, And to his honour leave't to set thee free Or hold thee bound. Thy father will be by!

SCENE III. - The Banqueting' Room.

[Enter MASTER WALTER and MASTER HEARTWELL.]

Heart. Thanks, Master Walter! Ne'er was child more bent To do her father's will, you'll own, than mine: Yet never one more froward.

Wal. All runs fair - Fair may all end! To-day you'll learn the cause That took me out of town. But soft a while, - Here comes the bridegroom, with his friends, and here The all-obedient bride.

[Enter on one hand JULIA, and on the other hand LORD ROCHDALE with LORD TINSEL and friends - afterwards CLIFFORD.]

Roch. Is she not fair?

Tin. She'll do. Your servant, lady! Master Walter, We're glad to see you. Sirs, you're welcome all. What wait they for? Are we to wed or not? We're ready - why don't they present the bride? I hope they know she is to wed an earl.

Roch. Should I speak first?

Tin. Not for your coronet! I, as your friend, may make

the first advance. We've come here to be married. Where's the bride?

Wal. There stands she, lord; if 'tis her will to wed, His lordship's free to take her.

Tin. Not a step! I, as your friend, may lead her to your lordship. Fair lady, by your leave.

Julia. No! not to you.

Tin. I ask your hand to give it to his lordship.

Julia. Nor to his lordship - save he will accept My hand without my heart! but I'll present My knee to him, and, by his lofty rank, Implore him now to do a lofty deed Will lift its stately head above his rank, - Assert him nobler yet in worth than name, - And, in the place of an unwilling bride, Unto a willing debt or make him lord, - Whose thanks shall be his vassals, night and day That still shall wait upon him!

Tin. What means this?

Julia. What is't behoves a wife to bring her lord?

Wal. A whole heart, and a true one.

Julia. I have none! Not half a heart - the fraction of a heart! Am I a woman it befits to wed?

Wal. Why, where's thy heart?

Julia. Gone - out of my keeping! Lost, past recovery: right and title to it - And all given up! and he that's owner on't, So fit to wear it, were it fifty hearts, I'd give it to him all!

Wal. Thou dost not mean His lordship's secretary?

Julia. Yes. Away Disguises! in that secretary know
The master of the heart, of which the poor, Unvalued, empty casket, at your feet - Its jewel gone - I now despairing throw!

[Kneels.]

Of his lord's bride he's lord! lord paramount! To whom her virgin homage first she paid, - 'Gainst whom rebelled in frowardness alone, Nor knew herself how loyal to him, till Another claimed her duty - then awoke To sense of all she owed him - all his worth - And all her undeservings!

Tin. Lady, we came not here to treat of hearts, - But marriage; which, so please you, is with us A simple joining, by the priest, of hands. A ring's put on, a prayer or two is said; You're man and wife, - and nothing more! For hearts, We oftener do without, than with them, lady!

Clif. So does not wed this lady!

Tin. Who are you?

Clif. I'm secretary to the Earl of Rochdale.

Tin. My lord!

Roch. I know him not -

Tin. I know him now - Your lordship's rival! Once Sir

Thomas Clifford.

Clif. Yes, and the bridegroom of that lady then, Then loved her - loves her still!

Julia. Was loved by her - Though then she knew it not! - is loved by her, As now she knows, and all the world may know!

Tin. We can't be laughed at. We are here to wed, And shall fulfil our contract.

Julia. Clifford!

Clif. Julia! You will not give your hand?

[A pause. JULIA seems utterly lost.]

Wal. You have forgot Again. You have a father!

Julia. Bring him now, - To see thy Julia justify thy training, And lay her life down to redeem her word!

Wal. And so redeems her all! Is it your will, My lord, these nuptials should go on?

Roch. It is.

Wal. Then is it mine they stop!

Tin. I told your lordship You should not keep a Hunchback for your agent.

Wal. Thought like my father, my good lord, who said He would not have a Hunchback for his son - So do I pardon you the savage slight. My lord, that I am not as straight as you, Was blemish neither of my thought nor will, My head nor heart. It was no act of mine. - Yet did it curdle Nature's kindly milk E'en where 'tis richest - in a parent's breast - To cast me out to heartless fosterage, Nor heartless always, as it proved - and give My portion to another! the same blood - But I'll be sworn, in vein, my lord, and soul - Although his trunk did swerve no more than yours - Not half so straight as I.

Tin. Upon my life You've got a modest agent, Rochdale! Now He'll prove himself descended - mark my words - From some small gentleman

Wal. And so you thought, Where Nature played the churl, it would be fit That fortune played it too. You would have had My lord absolve me of my agency! Fair lord, the flaw did cost me fifty times - A hundred times my agency:- but all's Recovered. Look, my lord, a testament To make a pension of his lordship's rent-roll! It is my father's, and was left by him, In case his heir should die without a son, Then to be opened. Heaven did send a son To bless the heir. Heaven took its gift away, He died - his father died. And Master Walter - The unsightly agent of his lordship there - The Hunchback whom your lordship would have stripped Of his agency - is now the Earl of Rochdale!

Tin. We've made a small mistake here. Never mind, 'Tis nothing in a lord.

Julia. The Earl of Rochdale!

Wal. And what of that? Thou know'st not half my greatness! A prouder title, Julia, have I yet, Sooner than part with which I'd give that up, And be again plain Master Walter. What! Dost thou not apprehend me? Yes, thou dost! Command thyself; don't gasp. My pupil - daughter! Come to thy father's heart!

[JULIA rushes into his arms.]

[Enter FATHOM.]

Fath. Thievery! Elopement - escape - arrest!

Wal. What's the matter?

Fath. Mistress Helen is running away with Master Modus - Master Modus is running away with Mistress Helen - but we have caught them, secured them, and here they come, to receive the reward of their merits.

[Enter HELEN and MODUS, followed by Servants.]

Helen. I'll ne'er wed man, if not my cousin Modus.

Mod. Nor woman I, save cousin Helen's she.

Wal. [To MASTER HEARTWELL.] A daughter, have you, and a nephew, too, Without their match in duty! Let them marry. For you, sir, who to-day have lost an earldom, Yet would have shared that earldom with my child - My only one - content yourself with prospect Of the succession; it must fall to you, And fit yourself to grace it. Ape not those Who rank by pride. The man of simplest bearing Is yet a lord, when he's a lord indeed! Tin. The paradox is obsolete. Ne'er heed! Learn from his book, and practise out of mine!

Wal. Sir Thomas Clifford, take my daughter's hand! If now you know the master of her heart! Give it, my

Julia! You suspect, I see, And rightly, there has been some masking here. Content thee, daughter, thou shalt know anon, How jealousy of my mis-shapen back Made me mistrustful of a child's affections - Who doubted e'en a wife's - so that I dropped The title of thy father, lest thy duty Should pay the debt thy love could solve alone. All this and more, that to thy friends and thee Pertains, at fitting time thou shalt be told. But now thy nuptials wait - the happy close Of thy hard trial - wholesome, though severe! The world won't cheat thee now - thy heart is proved; - Thou know'st thy peace by finding out its bane, And ne'er will act from reckless impulse more!

www.ingramcontent.com/pod-product-compliance
Lightning Source LLC
Chambersburg PA
CBHW032010040426
42448CB00006B/559